I0020989

Thank you for selecting this book as a valuable source of knowledge and inspiration. Our aim is to provide you with insights and information that will enrich your understanding and enhance your personal growth. We appreciate your decision to embark on this journey of discovery with us, and we hope that this book will exceed your expectations and leave a lasting impact on your life.

Title: Grinding for Gold
Subtitle: Play-to-Earn Gaming from Ponzi to Profession

Author: Alexander J. Clarke

Table of Contents

Introduction 7

Defining play-to-earn gaming and its core principles 7

*Brief History of Digital Economies and Ownership in Games*10

Overview of Blockchain Technology Enabling Play-to-Earn .13

The Promise and Vision of Open, User-Owned Economies 17

Chapter 1 - The Origins of Play-to-Earn 21

Early Digital Economies in Gaming 21

The Invention of Bitcoin and Blockchain Technology 24

Emergence of Non-Fungible Tokens (NFTs) 28

Rise of Blockchain-Based Games like CryptoKitties 32

Development of Early Play-to-Earn Game Prototypes 36

Chapter 2 - Axie Infinity and the First Wave 41

Overview of Axie Infinity's Game Design and Economics 41

Explosive Growth of Axie Infinity in the Philippines and
Beyond 46

Other Notable First-Generation Play-to-Earn Games 51

Attracting Venture Capital and Mainstream Attention 56

Limitations and Criticisms of Early Play-to-Earn Models 61

Chapter 3 - Challenges and Growing Pains 66

Collapses of Major Projects Like Uplandme Due to Flawed
Incentives 66

Lack of Fun and Engaging Gameplay Beyond Basic Grinding
.... 70

Pyramid Scheme Dynamics and Reliance on New Players 75

Market Declines and Loss of Interest Among Early Adopters 81

Questions about Longevity and Limiting Factors 87

Chapter 4 - Tokenomics and Blockchain Evolution ...93

Experimentation with New Token Models like Trove's Dual
Token System 93

Attempts to Improve Sustainability and Manage Inflation ... 98

Integration with Layer 2 Networks like ImmutableX for Scalability...103

Leveraging Decentralized Finance (DeFi) Protocols and DAO Structures.. 108

Contributions and Limitations of Blockchain Technology.... 113

Chapter 5 - Improving Gameplay and Design **119**

Developing More Compelling Gameplay Mechanics and Genres... 119

Focus on Casual Gamers vs. Just Crypto Natives 124

Allowing True Ownership of Assets via NFTs 129

Creating Vibrant Virtual Worlds and Communities 134

Balancing Playability and Earnings Potential.....................139

Chapter 6 - Guilds and the Player Ecosystem **144**

The Role and Operations of Scholar and Player Guilds........144

Providing Access and Education to New Crypto Users..........149

Economics and Profit-Sharing Models Between Guilds and Players..154

Controversies Around Potential Exploitation.....................159

How Guilds Contribute to Ecosystem Growth.....................164

Chapter 7 - Real-World Impacts **169**

Socio-Economic Influence in Developing Countries like the Philippines...169

Issues like Addiction, Unethical Play, and Educational Neglect 174

Regulatory Responses from Various Global Jurisdictions ...178

Mainstream Perceptions and Media Narratives..................183

Grassroots Player Stories and Testimonials 188

Chapter 8 - Institutional Investment and Adoption. 192

Crypto Funds Investing Hundreds of Millions in Play-to-Earn Networks 192

Large Game Studios like Ubisoft and Atari Entering the Play-to-Earn Market 196

Partnerships with Global Brands like Adidas, Samsung, and Others: The Symbiosis of Play-to-Earn and Corporate Giants *201*

Mass Media and Entertainment's Fascination: Play-to-Earn in Movies, Documentaries, and Beyond................................. 205

Celebrities as Catalysts: Play-to-Earn Thrust into the Spotlight 209

Chapter 9 - User Experience and Accessibility 213

Breaking Barriers: Custodial Wallets and Fiat On-Ramps in Play-to-Earn 213

Guiding the Way: Enhancing User Onboarding in Play-to-Earn Gaming.. 217

Mobile Empowerment: Play-to-Earn On the Go.................221

The Impact of UX and Visual Design Enhancements........... 225

Localization and translation for Global Audiences.............. 230

Chapter 10 - The Future of Play-to-Earn Gaming.....235

Envisioning Billions of Mainstream, Casual Gamers in the Future 235

Exploring the Future of Play-to-Earn with VR/AR Integration and New Gaming Genres.. 240

The Promise of Interoperability in Play-to-Earn Gaming's Metaverse Evolution 245

The Rise of User-Generated Content and Creator Economies in Play-to-Earn Gaming 250

The Evolution of Ownership, Governance, and Incentives in Play-to-Earn Gaming 255

Conclusion.. 260

Key Lessons and Insights from the Evolution of Play-to-Earn Gaming.. 260

Assessing the State of Play-to-Earn Adoption and Overcoming Hurdles.. 265

Predictions for the Future Maturation of Play-to-Earn Economies *269*

Broader Influence on Gaming, Online Communities, and Creator Incentives *273*

Concluding Thoughts on Play-to-Earn's Revolutionary Potential *277*

Wordbook **281**

Supplementary Materials **284**

Introduction
Defining play-to-earn gaming and its core principles

In the digital landscape, where virtual worlds and blockchain technologies intersect, a revolutionary concept has taken center stage - play-to-earn gaming. This introduction aims to dissect the very essence of play-to-earn gaming, laying the groundwork for a comprehensive exploration of its evolution, challenges, and future possibilities.

Play-to-Earn Gaming Unveiled

Play-to-earn gaming represents a paradigm shift in the traditional gaming industry. Unlike conventional games where players invest time and skill purely for entertainment, play-to-earn introduces a novel concept: the ability to earn tangible rewards, often in the form of cryptocurrency or digital assets, by engaging in gameplay. This transformative model challenges the notion that gaming is solely a recreational pursuit and introduces economic incentives that blur the lines between virtual and real-world value.

Core Principles at Play

At the heart of play-to-earn gaming lie several fundamental principles that define its structure and operation:

1. Ownership and Digital Assets: Play-to-earn hinges on the concept of true ownership. In traditional games, in-game assets are typically owned and controlled by the game developers. Contrastingly, play-to-earn games utilize blockchain and non-fungible tokens (NFTs) to grant players verifiable ownership of their in-game assets. This shift not only empowers players but also introduces the concept of a player-driven economy.

2. Tokenomics and Cryptocurrency Integration: Central to play-to-earn is the integration of cryptocurrency and token economics. Players earn native tokens or cryptocurrencies

within the game, creating a direct link between in-game achievements and real-world value. This financial layer adds a dynamic economic dimension to gaming, enabling players to trade, sell, or leverage their in-game assets beyond the confines of the gaming universe.

3. Decentralization and Blockchain Technology: Play-to-earn games leverage blockchain technology to decentralize control and eliminate intermediaries. This not only ensures transparency but also fosters trust among players. The immutable nature of blockchain records prevents fraud and facilitates a secure environment where players can confidently participate in an open and decentralized economy.

4. Incentive Mechanisms and Game Design: The success of play-to-earn hinges on creating engaging gameplay mechanics that seamlessly integrate with the economic model. Game designers must strike a delicate balance between providing an enjoyable gaming experience and offering lucrative earning opportunities. The design of incentives, challenges, and progression systems plays a pivotal role in attracting and retaining a diverse player base.

5. Community and Collaboration: Unlike traditional gaming ecosystems, play-to-earn emphasizes community collaboration. Players often form guilds or alliances, working collectively to optimize their earnings and navigate the challenges within the game. The collaborative aspect extends beyond the virtual realm, with players actively contributing to the growth and sustainability of the overall ecosystem.

As we embark on this exploration of play-to-earn gaming, each of these core principles will be dissected and examined in detail. From the foundations of ownership and blockchain technology to the intricacies of tokenomics and game design, the subsequent chapters will unravel the evolution of play-to-earn, shedding light on its triumphs, trials, and transformative potential.

Brief History of Digital Economies and Ownership in Games

To comprehend the revolutionary impact of play-to-earn gaming, it is imperative to embark on a journey through the annals of digital history, exploring the evolution of virtual economies and the concept of ownership within gaming realms. This historical overview sets the stage for understanding the roots from which play-to-earn gaming emerged and how it has reshaped the very foundations of gaming economics.

The Dawn of Virtual Economies

The concept of digital economies traces its roots back to the early days of online gaming. As multiplayer online games gained popularity in the late 20th century, players started interacting in shared virtual spaces. It didn't take long for game developers to recognize the potential for creating in-game economies, where players could buy, sell, and trade virtual goods. Games like "Ultima Online" and "EverQuest" pioneered this shift, introducing the notion that items and currencies within a game could hold intrinsic value.

The Birth of In-Game Currencies

As online gaming continued to evolve, in-game currencies emerged as a crucial component of virtual economies. Titles like "World of Warcraft" introduced the concept of gold as a digital currency, creating a medium for transactions within the game. This marked a significant departure from the earlier barter systems, paving the way for the establishment of digital marketplaces and player-driven economies.

Challenges of Centralized Ownership

However, the early digital economies were not without challenges. Centralized control of in-game assets by developers led to issues of ownership and trust. Players faced the risk of losing their hard-earned virtual possessions if a game was discontinued or if developers decided to alter the rules of ownership. This vulnerability spurred a desire for a more decentralized and player-centric approach.

The Rise of Blockchain Technology

The turning point in the evolution of digital ownership came with the advent of blockchain technology. The introduction of Bitcoin in 2009 demonstrated the potential for decentralized, transparent, and secure digital transactions. The underlying blockchain infrastructure offered a solution to the long-standing issues of ownership in traditional online games.

Non-Fungible Tokens (NFTs) and True Ownership

The breakthrough moment arrived with the development of non-fungible tokens (NFTs) on blockchain platforms. NFTs, which represent unique and indivisible digital assets, became a game-changer in the world of gaming. Unlike traditional in-game assets, NFTs provided true ownership to players, recorded on an immutable blockchain. This breakthrough laid the foundation for play-to-earn gaming, where players could possess, trade, and monetize their in-game assets beyond the confines of a single game.

Pioneering Projects and Proof of Concept

The convergence of blockchain and gaming principles paved the way for pioneering projects that experimented with decentralized ownership and player-driven economies. Early experiments, such as "Cryptokitties," allowed users to collect, breed, and trade unique virtual cats as NFTs, showcasing the potential for blockchain in creating verifiable digital scarcity and ownership.

The Precursor to Play-to-Earn Gaming

The seeds planted by these early projects set the stage for the emergence of play-to-earn gaming. The fusion of blockchain's decentralized architecture, NFTs, and the innate desire for true ownership laid the groundwork for a new era where players could not only own their in-game assets but also earn tangible rewards for their time and skills.

In the subsequent chapters, we will delve deeper into the specific milestones and key developments that propelled the gaming industry from centralized ownership models to the decentralized and player-centric economies exemplified by play-to-earn gaming. The journey through this historical landscape will illuminate the challenges, triumphs, and paradigm shifts that have shaped the course of digital economies within the gaming sphere.

Overview of Blockchain Technology Enabling Play-to-Earn

In the ever-evolving landscape of gaming, a technological marvel has emerged as the backbone of a revolutionary paradigm shift - blockchain. This section provides a comprehensive exploration of how blockchain technology serves as the catalyst for the rise of play-to-earn gaming. From decentralized ledgers to smart contracts, the elements of blockchain converge to redefine ownership, transparency, and incentives within virtual worlds.

Foundations of Blockchain

Blockchain, at its core, is a decentralized and distributed ledger technology. Originally conceptualized as the underlying infrastructure for cryptocurrencies like Bitcoin, its principles have transcended the realm of finance to permeate various industries, with gaming being one of the most transformative beneficiaries.

Decentralization: The essence of blockchain lies in its decentralized nature. Unlike traditional gaming architectures where a central authority governs all transactions, a blockchain operates on a peer-to-peer network. This decentralized model ensures that no single entity holds absolute control, fostering trust and transparency among participants.

Immutability: The immutability of blockchain records is a critical feature. Once information is added to the blockchain, it becomes practically impossible to alter. This immutability safeguards the integrity of in-game assets and transactions, mitigating the risk of fraud or manipulation.

Transparency: Every transaction recorded on the blockchain is transparent and accessible to all participants. This transparency not only enhances the security of the gaming ecosystem but also empowers players with visibility into the game's inner workings.

Smart Contracts and Programmable Assets

One of the cornerstones of blockchain technology contributing to play-to-earn gaming is the concept of smart contracts. These self-executing contracts, encoded with predefined rules and conditions, automate processes without the need for intermediaries. In the context of gaming, smart contracts enable the creation of programmable assets, dictating the rules of ownership, transfers, and rewards.

Tokenization: Blockchain facilitates the creation of fungible and non-fungible tokens (NFTs). Fungible tokens, often used as in-game currencies, are interchangeable, while NFTs represent unique, indivisible assets. Through tokenization, blockchain introduces a level of granularity to in-game assets, allowing each item to be distinct and ownable.

Ownership and True Scarcity: Smart contracts and tokenization address the long-standing challenge of ownership in gaming. Players, armed with NFTs, attain true ownership of in-game assets. The scarcity of these assets is not merely artificial; it is encoded into the blockchain, ensuring that digital items possess a rarity akin to physical collectibles.

Decentralized Finance (DeFi) and Play-to-Earn

The synergy between blockchain and decentralized finance (DeFi) further amplifies the play-to-earn model. DeFi protocols enable the creation of complex financial instruments, lending, and borrowing mechanisms within the gaming ecosystem.

Liquidity Pools: DeFi platforms introduce liquidity pools that allow players to stake their in-game assets, providing liquidity to the ecosystem. In return, players receive a share of transaction fees, adding an additional layer of earning potential.

Decentralized Autonomous Organizations (DAOs): DAOs, governed by smart contracts, empower players to participate in decision-making processes regarding the development and evolution of the game. This democratization of governance aligns with the principles of play-to-earn, where the community actively shapes the gaming experience.

Layer 2 Solutions for Scalability

As the popularity of play-to-earn gaming grows, scalability becomes a paramount consideration. Layer 2 solutions, built on top of the main blockchain, address scalability issues by conducting transactions off-chain or via side chains.

ImmutableX and Scalable NFTs: Platforms like ImmutableX utilize layer 2 scaling solutions to enhance the scalability of NFTs. By settling transactions off-chain and committing only the essential data to the blockchain, these solutions optimize the gaming experience without compromising security or decentralization.

The Promise of Interoperability

Interoperability is a key promise of blockchain technology in the context of play-to-earn gaming. The ability for in-game assets to transcend individual games and even virtual worlds creates a seamless, interconnected metaverse.

Cross-Game Assets: Blockchain's interoperability enables players to use their assets across different games, breaking down the silos that traditionally confined in-game economies. This opens avenues for cross-game collaboration and the creation of expansive player-driven universes.

The Transformative Potential of Blockchain in Gaming

As we delve into the subsequent chapters, each facet of blockchain's contribution to play-to-earn gaming will be meticulously examined. From its role in enabling true ownership to the intricate dance of smart contracts and DeFi, blockchain technology stands as the linchpin of a gaming revolution. As we unravel the complexities and nuances, a clearer picture will emerge of how blockchain not only enables play-to-earn but reshapes the very essence of digital entertainment.

The Promise and Vision of Open, User-Owned Economies

In the realm of traditional gaming, the concept of ownership has long been a fleeting illusion, confined within the virtual boundaries dictated by game developers. However, with the advent of blockchain technology and the rise of play-to-earn gaming, a profound promise emerges - the vision of open, user-owned economies. This section delves into the transformative potential of liberating digital assets, decentralizing economies, and empowering players as active contributors to the virtual worlds they inhabit.

Liberating Digital Assets: From Pixels to Property

In the early days of gaming, the notion of owning in-game assets was akin to possessing ephemeral pixels on a screen. Items, currencies, and achievements, while earned through time and skill, remained under the centralized control of game developers. The promise of open, user-owned economies disrupts this paradigm by imbuing digital assets with tangible value and genuine ownership.

Verifiable Scarcity and Ownership: Blockchain's introduction of non-fungible tokens (NFTs) revolutionized the perception of digital assets. Each NFT, representing a unique and irreplaceable item, is securely recorded on an immutable blockchain, providing players with verifiable scarcity and true ownership. The promise lies in the liberation of assets from the confines of individual games, allowing players to possess, trade, and monetize their virtual possessions across diverse gaming ecosystems.

Eradicating the Ephemeral: The promise of open, user-owned economies confronts the ephemeral nature of digital assets in traditional gaming. In this new paradigm, a player's virtual sword, earned through countless battles, transcends the boundaries of a single game and becomes a lasting, tradable entity, fostering a sense of permanence and value in the digital realm.

Decentralizing Economies: Empowering the Players

Centralized control over in-game economies has historically stifled player agency and limited the potential for genuine economic participation. The promise of open, user-owned economies is rooted in the decentralization of economic structures, placing the power to shape, influence, and benefit from the gaming economy squarely in the hands of players.

Player-Driven Value Creation: In traditional gaming, value creation is a unilateral process dictated by developers. In contrast, open, user-owned economies empower players to actively contribute to the creation of value within the gaming ecosystem. The actions, decisions, and interactions of players directly influence the economic landscape, fostering a dynamic environment where the community becomes an integral part of economic evolution.

Incentivizing Collaboration: The promise of decentralized economies lies in the incentive structures that reward collaboration and contribution. Through mechanisms like play-to-earn and decentralized autonomous organizations (DAOs), players are not only rewarded for their individual efforts but are also encouraged to collaborate, collectively steering the course of the gaming economy. This collaborative approach fosters a sense of shared ownership and responsibility among the gaming community.

Empowering Players as Stakeholders: A Vision of Inclusivity

The vision of open, user-owned economies extends beyond economic participation, aiming to transform players from mere consumers into stakeholders with a vested interest in the virtual worlds they inhabit.

Democratizing Decision-Making: Traditional gaming often relegates decision-making power to a select few within development studios. In the promise of open economies, the vision is one of democratization, where players have a direct say in the evolution of the game. DAOs, governed by smart contracts, enable decentralized decision-making, allowing the gaming community to collectively shape the rules, features, and future developments.

Inclusive Participation: The vision of open, user-owned economies champions inclusivity, breaking down barriers that traditionally limited player participation. Regardless of geographic location, socio-economic status, or gaming background, players become active participants and contributors to the economic and creative aspects of the virtual worlds they inhabit. This inclusivity not only enriches the gaming experience but also fosters diverse and vibrant player communities.

Closing the Divide Between Virtual and Real: A Revolutionary Vision

The promise and vision of open, user-owned economies transcend the digital realm, challenging the dichotomy between the virtual and the real. By instilling genuine value, ownership, and economic agency in the hands of players, this vision represents a radical departure from traditional gaming norms.

Blurring Virtual and Real Wealth: Open, user-owned economies hold the promise of blurring the lines between virtual and real-world wealth. Digital assets, earned and owned within the gaming ecosystem, can be traded, sold, and leveraged in real-world contexts, creating a bridge between the two realms. This vision not only transforms gaming into a potentially lucrative pursuit but also introduces new possibilities for economic empowerment.

Revolutionizing the Creator-Player Relationship: Traditionally, the creator-player relationship has been one-sided, with game developers holding the reins of power. The vision of open economies redefines this relationship, turning players into active contributors, collaborators, and even creators within the gaming ecosystem. The divide between game developers and players diminishes, giving rise to a symbiotic relationship where both parties share in the successes and evolution of the virtual worlds they coalesce to create.

Navigating the Landscape of Promise and Vision

As we embark on an exploration of open, user-owned economies in the chapters that follow, the intricacies, challenges, and triumphs of this transformative vision will be unveiled. From the liberation of digital assets to the democratization of decision-making, the promise of open economies signifies a profound shift in the dynamics of gaming. It is a journey into uncharted territory, where the intersection of blockchain technology and gaming ideology converges to redefine not only how we play but how we perceive, value, and participate in the vast landscapes of virtual worlds.

Chapter 1 - The Origins of Play-to-Earn
Early Digital Economies in Gaming

The inception of play-to-earn gaming finds its roots in the early days of digital economies within online gaming. This chapter delves into the formative years when players first began to recognize the value of their in-game assets, setting the stage for the transformative concept of earning tangible rewards through virtual endeavors.

The Dawn of Multiplayer Online Games:

The evolution of digital economies began in earnest with the rise of multiplayer online games in the late 20th century. Games like "Ultima Online" and "EverQuest" pioneered the concept of persistent virtual worlds where players interacted in real-time. This newfound connectivity laid the groundwork for the emergence of player-driven economies.

Virtual Goods and Currency: As players traversed these virtual realms, they accumulated digital goods and currencies. Virtual swords, armor, and other in-game items started to hold a perceived value, and players began to trade these assets with one another. Although the transactions were informal and often occurred outside the game's mechanics, they hinted at the economic potential within the virtual space.

The Birth of In-Game Economies:

The late 1990s witnessed the formalization of in-game economies, where game developers recognized and integrated virtual currencies into the gaming experience. Games like "Diablo II" introduced the concept of trading items for in-game gold, paving the way for a more structured virtual economy. This marked the beginning of a transition from ad-hoc player trading to intentional economic design by game developers.

Marketplaces and Trade Hubs: As in-game economies evolved, dedicated marketplaces and trade hubs emerged within games. These spaces facilitated player-to-player transactions, providing a platform for buying and selling virtual goods. The existence of these hubs emphasized the demand for player-driven economies and hinted at the latent desire for true ownership of in-game assets.

Gold Farming and Third-Party Markets:

The demand for virtual goods gave rise to a unique phenomenon known as gold farming. In games like "World of Warcraft," entrepreneurial players engaged in repetitive tasks to accumulate in-game currency or items, which they then sold to other players for real-world money. Simultaneously, third-party markets outside the confines of the game flourished, connecting buyers and sellers in a burgeoning digital marketplace.

Emergence of Real-World Value: The practice of gold farming injected a real-world monetary value into virtual assets. Players were willing to pay for in-game currency or items, recognizing the time and effort saved by acquiring these assets through external transactions. This marked a crucial shift in perception, as virtual goods began to be perceived not only as items of entertainment but as commodities with economic value.

Challenges of Centralized Ownership:

Despite the economic strides made within digital economies, the fundamental challenge remained - centralized ownership. In traditional gaming models, developers retained absolute control over in-game assets. This centralization created vulnerabilities, as players faced the risk of losing their digital possessions if a game was discontinued or if developers altered the rules of ownership.

Limitations of Central Control: The limitations of centralized control became apparent as developers wielded unchecked authority over the fate of in-game assets. This lack of player agency sparked a desire for a more decentralized and player-centric approach to ownership.

Seeds of Decentralization:

The early years of digital economies sowed the seeds of decentralization, setting the stage for the disruptive influence of blockchain technology. Players, now accustomed to the idea of virtual ownership and trading, yearned for a system that would provide true ownership, security, and transparency.

Player Activism and Advocacy: Player communities began to advocate for changes in ownership models. Instances of game developers altering or revoking in-game items fueled a sense of urgency among players to seek alternatives that could provide a more equitable and secure system.

Towards a Decentralized Future:

As the first chapter of this exploration into the origins of play-to-earn gaming concludes, the narrative unfolds at a pivotal moment. The desire for true ownership and decentralized control of in-game assets becomes a beacon, guiding the industry towards a future where players not only participate in economies but become architects of virtual worlds. The seeds planted in the early digital economies germinate, pointing the way to a transformative era where play-to-earn takes center stage.

The Invention of Bitcoin and Blockchain Technology

The narrative of play-to-earn gaming intertwines with a groundbreaking technological innovation - the invention of Bitcoin and blockchain technology. In this chapter, we delve into the genesis of these revolutionary concepts, exploring how they laid the foundation for the transformative intersection of blockchain and gaming economies.

Bitcoin: A Pioneering Cryptocurrency

The journey begins with the enigmatic figure or group known as Satoshi Nakamoto, who, in 2008, introduced the world to Bitcoin, a peer-to-peer electronic cash system. Bitcoin represented a departure from traditional financial systems, utilizing decentralized ledger technology to enable secure, transparent, and censorship-resistant transactions.

Decentralization and Trustlessness: Bitcoin's core innovation lay in its decentralized nature. By leveraging a distributed network of nodes, Bitcoin eliminated the need for a central authority, introducing trustless transactions where participants did not need to rely on intermediaries like banks. This decentralized architecture, powered by a technology called blockchain, became the bedrock of a new era.

Immutable Ledger: The blockchain, a chain of blocks containing transactional data, provided an immutable record of all transactions. Once added to the blockchain, transactions became irreversible, ensuring transparency and integrity. This innovation addressed the double-spending problem that had previously hindered the creation of digital currencies.

The Emergence of Blockchain Technology:

Bitcoin's success paved the way for the broader exploration of blockchain technology. Beyond its application in financial systems, developers and innovators recognized its potential to disrupt various industries, including the gaming sector. Blockchain's decentralized, transparent, and secure properties hinted at a solution to the challenges that had long plagued digital economies within games.

Decentralized Ownership and True Scarcity: The concept of non-fungible tokens (NFTs) emerged as a direct application of blockchain technology within the gaming space. NFTs represented unique, indivisible assets that could be tokenized and securely recorded on the blockchain. This introduced the novel concept of true ownership, where players had verifiable proof of ownership for their in-game assets. The scarcity of these assets was no longer subject to the whims of developers but encoded into the blockchain, introducing a new era of digital ownership.

Blockchain Meets Gaming: The Genesis of Play-to-Earn

As blockchain technology gained traction, the intersection with gaming became inevitable. Innovators recognized the potential to revolutionize digital economies within games by integrating blockchain principles. This convergence marked the genesis of play-to-earn gaming.

Smart Contracts and Programmable Assets: Smart contracts, self-executing code on the blockchain, became instrumental in shaping the play-to-earn model. These programmable assets enabled the creation of dynamic, rule-based systems that governed ownership, transfers, and rewards within games. The fusion of smart contracts and NFTs allowed for the creation of in-game assets that could be owned, traded, and monetized in a secure and transparent environment.

Bitcoin's Influence on Digital Ownership:

Bitcoin's influence extended beyond its role as a digital currency. Its decentralized ethos, emphasis on ownership, and resistance to censorship inspired a broader movement toward reimagining ownership within digital realms.

Philosophy of Decentralization: Bitcoin's philosophy of decentralization and financial sovereignty resonated with a growing community of players who sought autonomy over their in-game assets. The principles of decentralization became a rallying cry for digital ownership advocates, setting the stage for a paradigm shift in how players perceived the value and control of their virtual possessions.

Blockchain as the Backbone of Play-to-Earn Gaming:

Blockchain technology emerged as the backbone of play-to-earn gaming, providing the infrastructure for decentralized ownership, transparent transactions, and innovative economic models. The fusion of Bitcoin's foundational principles and blockchain's capabilities opened the door to a new era where players could not only participate in digital economies but truly own and derive tangible value from their virtual endeavors.

Security and Transparency: Blockchain's security features ensured the integrity of in-game assets, mitigating the risks of fraud or manipulation. Transactions became transparent, visible to all participants on the blockchain, fostering a trustless environment that aligned with the ethos of play-to-earn.

Looking Ahead: The Impact of Bitcoin and Blockchain on Gaming:

As this chapter unfolds, it becomes evident that the invention of Bitcoin and the subsequent evolution of blockchain technology catalyzed a profound shift in the gaming landscape. The promise of true ownership, decentralized economies, and the convergence of digital and real-world value became the guiding lights for the pioneers of play-to-earn gaming. The subsequent chapters will unravel how these foundational concepts ignited the spark that led to the flourishing ecosystem of play-to-earn, shaping the future of gaming in ways previously thought unimaginable.

Emergence of Non-Fungible Tokens (NFTs)

In the evolutionary timeline of play-to-earn gaming, a pivotal chapter unfolds with the emergence of Non-Fungible Tokens (NFTs). This section traces the roots of NFTs, exploring how these unique digital assets became a cornerstone in reshaping the landscape of ownership, authenticity, and value within virtual gaming realms.

From Fungibility to Uniqueness: The Concept of NFTs

The concept of fungibility, where each unit of a currency or asset is interchangeable with another of the same value, has been a fundamental characteristic of traditional currencies and many digital assets. NFTs disrupted this notion by introducing uniqueness and indivisibility. Each NFT represents a distinct, irreplaceable item, challenging the uniformity that defined digital assets in the gaming space.

Tokenization of Unique Assets: The tokenization of unique assets on the blockchain marked a paradigm shift. NFTs, built on blockchain protocols like Ethereum, allowed developers to create digital tokens representing singular entities, such as in-game items, characters, or pieces of virtual real estate. Each NFT, with its own distinct metadata, became a digital certificate of authenticity and ownership.

The Catalyst: CryptoKitties and the Birth of NFT Craze

The NFT revolution found its catalyst in the form of "CryptoKitties," an Ethereum-based game launched in 2017. In this game, players could buy, sell, and breed unique digital cats, with each cat represented as an NFT. The groundbreaking aspect was not merely the gameplay but the revelation that digital assets could possess intrinsic value and uniqueness, opening a new dimension in the world of digital ownership.

Scarce, Collectible, and Tradeable: CryptoKitties introduced the concept of true digital scarcity. Each

CryptoKitty, as an NFT, was scarce by design, and its value was determined by factors such as its uniqueness, rarity, and breeding lineage. Players engaged in a vibrant marketplace, trading CryptoKitties as digital collectibles, creating a fervor around the potential value of unique digital assets.

Beyond Gaming: NFTs in the Art World

The CryptoKitties phenomenon sparked wider interest in the concept of NFTs, extending beyond the gaming community. Artists and creators recognized the potential to tokenize and sell digital art as NFTs, introducing a novel revenue stream for creators in the digital age. The art world witnessed a paradigm shift as digital art, previously plagued by issues of reproducibility, found a way to be owned and valued through NFTs.

Digital Scarcity in Art: NFTs brought digital scarcity to the art world, allowing artists to create limited editions of their digital work. Each NFT served as a certificate of authenticity, ensuring that collectors owned a unique and verifiable piece of digital art. The transparency and immutability of the blockchain addressed concerns of provenance and ownership in the realm of digital creativity.

NFT Standards and Interoperability:

The success of NFTs prompted the establishment of standards to ensure interoperability and widespread adoption. The most notable standard is the ERC-721, which outlines the basic rules for creating NFTs on the Ethereum blockchain. This standardization enabled the seamless creation and interaction of NFTs across various platforms, laying the foundation for the vibrant NFT ecosystem that would later intersect with play-to-earn gaming.

Expanding the NFT Ecosystem: With standards in place, developers and creators began exploring diverse applications for NFTs, ranging from virtual goods and real estate to digital identity and intellectual property. The interoperability of NFTs across different platforms fostered a dynamic ecosystem where digital assets could transcend individual games and virtual environments.

Blockchain's Role in NFTs: Security and Authenticity

The inherent features of blockchain played a crucial role in the success of NFTs. Security, transparency, and authenticity, provided by the decentralized nature of blockchain, addressed key challenges in the digital asset space.

Security and Immutability: NFTs leverage the security of blockchain to protect against fraud and counterfeiting. Once an NFT is minted and recorded on the blockchain, its information is immutable, ensuring that the ownership history and attributes of the digital asset remain tamper-proof.

Transparent Ownership and Provenance: The transparency of blockchain ensures clear ownership records and provenance for NFTs. Potential buyers can verify the authenticity and ownership history of an NFT before making a purchase, addressing concerns related to digital asset provenance and ensuring that collectors have genuine, verifiable ownership.

NFTs and Gaming: Bridging the Virtual and Real Worlds

The convergence of NFTs and gaming became inevitable as the unique characteristics of NFTs addressed long-standing challenges within the gaming industry. The concept of true ownership, scarcity, and interoperability introduced by NFTs set the stage for the transformative integration of blockchain technology in play-to-earn gaming.

Digital Ownership in Gaming: NFTs brought the concept of true ownership to in-game assets. Players could now own, trade, and monetize their virtual possessions beyond the confines of individual games. This shift marked a departure from the traditional model where developers retained centralized control over in-game items.

Scarcity and Value Proposition: The scarcity embedded in NFTs introduced a new dimension to the perceived value of in-game assets. Rare, unique items represented by NFTs became sought after, creating a marketplace where players could derive real-world value from their virtual endeavors.

The Genesis of Play-to-Earn: NFTs Meet Blockchain Gaming

As NFTs gained traction, their integration with blockchain gaming laid the foundation for play-to-earn. Games began leveraging NFTs to represent in-game assets, allowing players to truly own, trade, and earn from their digital possessions. The subsequent chapters will unveil how this fusion of NFTs and blockchain gaming ushered in the era of play-to-earn, where the virtual and real worlds became interconnected through the transformative power of blockchain and unique digital assets.

Rise of Blockchain-Based Games like CryptoKitties

As the exploration of play-to-earn gaming unfolds, a significant chapter in its origins is marked by the rise of blockchain-based games, with CryptoKitties standing as a pioneering example. In this section, we delve into the genesis of CryptoKitties and the impact it had on shaping the narrative of ownership, digital scarcity, and the integration of blockchain technology within the gaming landscape.

Genesis of CryptoKitties: Unleashing Digital Collectibles on Blockchain

In the annals of blockchain-based games, CryptoKitties, launched in 2017, emerged as a groundbreaking experiment that would redefine the possibilities of digital ownership and scarcity within a decentralized ecosystem.

Unique Concept of Digital Collectibles: CryptoKitties introduced a unique concept — digital collectibles in the form of adorable, breedable, and tradable virtual cats. Each CryptoKitty, represented as a non-fungible token (NFT) on the Ethereum blockchain, possessed distinct attributes, such as color, pattern, and generation, making them truly one-of-a-kind.

Smart Contracts and Genetic Algorithm: At the heart of CryptoKitties was the utilization of smart contracts, self-executing code on the blockchain. These smart contracts governed the breeding process of CryptoKitties, implementing a genetic algorithm that determined the traits of the offspring. This not only added a layer of complexity to the game but also showcased the programmable nature of blockchain technology.

Digital Scarcity and Ownership: The CryptoKitties Frenzy

The allure of CryptoKitties lay in its introduction of digital scarcity and genuine ownership. Players could buy, sell, and breed their CryptoKitties, with each cat's unique traits contributing to its perceived value. The breeding mechanism introduced an element of chance, further enhancing the rarity and uniqueness of each CryptoKitty.

Marketplace Dynamics: The introduction of a marketplace allowed players to trade their CryptoKitties with one another. The marketplace became a bustling hub of activity, with CryptoKitties changing hands for varying amounts of cryptocurrency based on factors such as rarity, generation, and perceived aesthetic appeal. This marketplace dynamic highlighted the subjective and evolving nature of digital asset valuation.

Scalability Challenges: The immense popularity of CryptoKitties, however, exposed the scalability challenges of the Ethereum blockchain. As the game gained widespread adoption, it contributed to network congestion, slower transaction times, and higher fees. This experience underscored the need for scalable blockchain solutions, a theme that would later be addressed by subsequent iterations in the play-to-earn ecosystem.

CryptoKitties as a Cultural Phenomenon

Beyond its impact on the blockchain gaming landscape, CryptoKitties became a cultural phenomenon, reaching beyond the crypto community and captivating mainstream attention. The concept of owning and trading digital cats transcended the realm of gaming, infiltrating discussions on the future of digital ownership and the broader potential of blockchain technology.

Mainstream Recognition: CryptoKitties garnered attention from mainstream media outlets, introducing blockchain gaming to audiences unfamiliar with the intricacies of cryptocurrency and decentralized technologies. The concept of owning and trading unique digital assets resonated with a broader demographic, sparking conversations about the evolving nature of ownership in the digital age.

Community Engagement and Creativity: The CryptoKitties community actively engaged with the game, fostering creativity and collaboration. Players organized events, created art inspired by their CryptoKitties, and built ancillary projects around the game. This vibrant community spirit contributed to the enduring legacy of CryptoKitties as more than just a game — it became a cultural touchstone in the narrative of blockchain-based experiences.

CryptoKitties as a Trailblazer: Lessons Learned

CryptoKitties, with its unprecedented success and cultural impact, served as a trailblazer in the exploration of blockchain-based games. The lessons learned from the CryptoKitties phenomenon laid the groundwork for subsequent projects within the play-to-earn space.

User Engagement and Community Building: One of the key takeaways from CryptoKitties was the importance of fostering user engagement and community building. The game's success was not solely attributed to its novel mechanics but also to the sense of community and creativity that flourished among its players.

Scarcity, Ownership, and Market Dynamics: CryptoKitties underscored the significance of introducing scarcity and genuine ownership within blockchain-based games. The game's marketplace dynamics highlighted the evolving nature of digital asset valuation and the subjective factors that contribute to the perceived value of virtual items.

Legacy of CryptoKitties: Influencing the Play-to-Earn Ecosystem

As the legacy of CryptoKitties reverberates through the gaming industry, its influence extends into the play-to-earn ecosystem. The concepts of digital scarcity, true ownership, and blockchain-based marketplaces, pioneered by CryptoKitties, laid the groundwork for a paradigm shift in how players perceive, interact with, and derive value from virtual assets.

Integration of NFTs and Smart Contracts: The success of CryptoKitties demonstrated the potential of integrating NFTs and smart contracts within gaming ecosystems. Play-to-earn games drew inspiration from CryptoKitties, incorporating these elements to provide players with true ownership and the ability to monetize their in-game assets.

Evolving Scalability Solutions: The scalability challenges faced by CryptoKitties prompted a broader conversation about the need for scalable blockchain solutions in gaming. Subsequent projects within the play-to-earn ecosystem explored various blockchain architectures and layer 2 solutions to address scalability issues, learning from CryptoKitties' experiences.

Conclusion: CryptoKitties as a Catalyst for Play-to-Earn Innovation

As this exploration of CryptoKitties unfolds, it becomes evident that this seemingly whimsical game played a profound role in catalyzing innovation within the play-to-earn ecosystem. The rise of blockchain-based games, exemplified by CryptoKitties, laid the foundation for a transformative era where players are not just participants but active contributors to the evolving narratives of digital ownership, scarcity, and value creation. The subsequent chapters will delve deeper into the ripple effects of CryptoKitties and how they paved the way for the broader play-to-earn revolution.

Development of Early Play-to-Earn Game Prototypes

In the evolutionary journey toward play-to-earn gaming, a crucial phase unfolds with the development of early prototypes that tested the waters of decentralized economies, true ownership, and the integration of blockchain technology. This section delves into the pioneering efforts that paved the way for the transformative concept of earning tangible rewards through virtual gameplay.

The Genesis: From Concept to Prototype

The initial steps toward play-to-earn gaming were experimental, as innovators sought to marry blockchain technology with gaming mechanics to create a novel economic model. This phase marked the birth of early play-to-earn game prototypes, where developers explored the possibilities of decentralized ownership and the integration of cryptocurrency within virtual ecosystems.

Blockchain's Promise: The promise of blockchain, with its decentralized and transparent nature, captivated developers looking to disrupt traditional gaming models. The idea of allowing players to truly own and trade in-game assets represented a paradigm shift, and early prototypes aimed to bring this vision to life.

Early Play-to-Earn Experiments: Lessons Learned

During this experimental phase, several projects emerged, each contributing to the understanding of the challenges and opportunities inherent in play-to-earn models. These early experiments served as valuable lessons that shaped the evolution of the broader play-to-earn ecosystem.

Decentralized Ownership: The core concept of play-to-earn revolves around decentralized ownership. Early prototypes grappled with the technical intricacies of implementing true ownership on the blockchain. Developers experimented with various blockchain protocols, exploring how to securely tokenize in-game assets and grant players verifiable ownership.

Economic Models: The development of play-to-earn prototypes involved the creation of new economic models. Developers sought to balance the in-game rewards with the broader cryptocurrency ecosystem, exploring tokenomics that incentivized player participation, skill development, and asset accumulation. These early economic models laid the groundwork for more sophisticated approaches in subsequent play-to-earn projects.

Rise of Cryptocurrency Integration: Early Tokenomics

As play-to-earn prototypes matured, the integration of cryptocurrency into gameplay mechanics became a focal point. These early forays into tokenomics explored ways to seamlessly integrate digital currencies within the gaming experience, establishing a direct link between in-game achievements and real-world value.

Cryptocurrency as Rewards: In early play-to-earn prototypes, cryptocurrency was introduced as a reward for specific in-game accomplishments. Players could earn tokens by completing quests, achieving milestones, or demonstrating skill within the virtual environment. This integration aimed to bridge the gap between the virtual and real-world value.

Emergence of Unique Tokens: Some prototypes experimented with the creation of unique in-game tokens on the blockchain. These tokens, often representing specific assets or achievements, could be traded both within and outside the game. The introduction of unique tokens laid the foundation for the concept of non-fungible tokens (NFTs) and their role in play-to-earn gaming.

Challenges Faced: Scalability, User Adoption, and Regulatory Uncertainty

The development of early play-to-earn game prototypes was not without its challenges. Innovators faced hurdles related to scalability, user adoption, and navigating regulatory uncertainty. These challenges, however, provided valuable insights that paved the way for improvements in subsequent iterations.

Scalability Issues: As player engagement increased, scalability issues on existing blockchain networks became apparent. Slow transaction times and high fees posed challenges to the seamless integration of cryptocurrency within gameplay. Early prototypes highlighted the need for scalable blockchain solutions to accommodate the growing demands of play-to-earn ecosystems.

User Adoption and Onboarding: Educating players about blockchain technology and cryptocurrency was a significant challenge. Early prototypes struggled with onboarding new users, requiring efforts to simplify the user experience, provide educational resources, and integrate custodial wallets to lower entry barriers.

Regulatory Uncertainty: The intersection of gaming and cryptocurrency raised regulatory questions, and early prototypes navigated uncertain terrain. Developers grappled with compliance issues, striving to strike a balance between innovation and adherence to evolving regulatory frameworks.

Evolution of Governance Models: DAOs and Community Involvement

The development of early play-to-earn game prototypes also witnessed experiments with decentralized autonomous organizations (DAOs) and community-driven governance models. These initiatives aimed to give players a more direct role in shaping the rules, policies, and future developments of the games they participated in.

DAOs and Decision-Making: Some early prototypes embraced the concept of DAOs, where community members could participate in governance by voting on key decisions. This decentralized approach to decision-making empowered players, fostering a sense of ownership and responsibility within the gaming community.

Community Feedback and Iterative Development: The inclusion of community feedback became a hallmark of early play-to-earn prototypes. Developers actively sought input from players to refine and iterate on game mechanics, economic models, and overall user experience. This iterative development process laid the foundation for collaborative game design within the play-to-earn paradigm.

Trailblazers and Influencers: The Ripple Effect

As the development of early play-to-earn game prototypes unfolded, certain projects emerged as trailblazers, influencing the trajectory of the entire ecosystem. These projects, whether successful or not, left an indelible mark on the evolution of play-to-earn gaming.

Success Stories and Lessons: Some early play-to-earn prototypes achieved notable success, demonstrating the viability of the model. These success stories provided valuable lessons for subsequent projects, shedding light on effective tokenomics, engaging gameplay mechanics, and community-driven development.

Innovative Mechanics and Features: Innovative features introduced in early prototypes, such as unique tokenization, dynamic economic models, and decentralized governance, became benchmarks for future play-to-earn endeavors. These pioneering mechanics inspired a wave of creativity and experimentation within the gaming and blockchain development communities.

Conclusion: Paving the Way for the Play-to-Earn Revolution

The development of early play-to-earn game prototypes represents a foundational chapter in the evolution of decentralized gaming economies. From humble experiments to trailblazing initiatives, these prototypes laid the groundwork for a transformative paradigm shift. The subsequent chapters will unveil how the insights gained from these early endeavors fueled the broader play-to-earn revolution, shaping an ecosystem where players not only play but actively contribute to the creation and evolution of virtual economies.

Chapter 2 - Axie Infinity and the First Wave
Overview of Axie Infinity's Game Design and Economics

Axie Infinity, a pioneering force in the play-to-earn gaming space, stands as a symbol of innovation, community-driven success, and economic empowerment. In this section, we delve into the intricacies of Axie Infinity's game design and economics, exploring how this blockchain-based game reshaped the landscape of digital ownership, decentralized economies, and the player-centric approach to gaming.

Foundations of Axie Infinity: A Play-to-Earn Ecosystem

Axie Infinity, developed by Sky Mavis, introduced a novel play-to-earn model that went beyond token rewards, reimagining the relationship between players and virtual assets. To understand the impact of Axie Infinity, it's crucial to dissect its game design and economic foundations.

Axies: The Heart of the Ecosystem: At the core of Axie Infinity are the Axies, adorable and fantastical creatures that players collect, breed, and battle. Each Axie is represented as a non-fungible token (NFT) on the Ethereum blockchain, providing players with true ownership and the ability to trade these digital assets both within and outside the game.

Play-to-Earn Dynamics: Earning SLP and AXS Tokens

Axie Infinity introduced a dual-token system, featuring Smooth Love Potion (SLP) and Axie Infinity Shards (AXS). These tokens serve as the economic drivers of the Axie ecosystem, and players can earn them through various in-game activities.

Smooth Love Potion (SLP): SLP is the primary utility token within Axie Infinity. Players earn SLP by participating in battles and completing various tasks. This token, initially designed to be a love potion for breeding Axies, became a tradable asset on external exchanges, allowing players to convert their in-game efforts into real-world value.

Axie Infinity Shards (AXS): AXS is the governance and utility token of the Axie Infinity ecosystem. Beyond its role in governance, AXS is used for staking, participating in token sales, and accessing premium features within the Axie universe. AXS represents a form of ownership in the broader Axie community, aligning the incentives of players with the success and growth of the entire ecosystem.

Battles, Breeding, and Economic Activity

Axie Infinity's game design is centered around turn-based battles and a unique breeding system. Understanding the dynamics of these core activities provides insights into the economic structures that sustain the play-to-earn model.

Battle Mechanics: Axie battles are a strategic and engaging aspect of the game. Players assemble a team of Axies, each with distinct abilities, and compete against other players or non-player characters (NPCs). Winning battles not only earns players SLP but also contributes to their ranking, opening up additional rewards.

Breeding System: Axie breeding adds a layer of complexity to the ecosystem. Players can breed two Axies to create a new one, with the offspring inheriting traits from its parents. The breeding process requires the use of SLP, introducing a sink for the token and creating economic incentives for players to engage in breeding activities.

Market Dynamics: Player-Driven Economy

Axie Infinity's marketplace is a bustling hub where players buy, sell, and trade Axies and in-game items. The player-driven economy, facilitated by blockchain technology, introduces a dynamic marketplace where the value of assets is determined by supply, demand, and perceived rarity.

Axie Marketplace: The Axie marketplace operates on decentralized exchanges, allowing players to list their Axies and items for sale. The marketplace dynamics are influenced by factors such as the scarcity of certain Axie traits, battle performance, and cosmetic features. This decentralized approach to trading aligns with the broader ethos of play-to-earn gaming, where players have control over their virtual assets.

Economic Empowerment: Axie Infinity's marketplace has become a source of economic empowerment for players, especially in regions with economic challenges. The ability to earn cryptocurrency through gameplay provides an alternative income stream, offering financial opportunities to individuals who might not have access to traditional forms of income.

Community and Collaboration: Guilds and Scholar Programs

Axie Infinity's success is intricately tied to the sense of community and collaboration it fosters. The introduction of guilds and scholar programs adds a layer of social and economic cohesion to the Axie ecosystem.

Guilds: Guilds within Axie Infinity are player-led communities that offer support, education, and collaboration. Guilds play a crucial role in onboarding new players, providing strategic guidance, and creating a sense of belonging within the broader Axie community. The collaborative nature of guilds contributes to the overall growth and sustainability of the Axie ecosystem.

Scholar Programs: Axie Infinity's scholar programs allow experienced players to lend their Axies to individuals who might not have the resources to own their Axies initially. Scholars play the game using these borrowed Axies and share the earned rewards with the Axie owner. This model promotes inclusivity, allowing more players to participate in the play-to-earn ecosystem.

Challenges and Iterative Development: Scalability and Gameplay

The success of Axie Infinity did not come without challenges. Scalability issues, particularly on the Ethereum blockchain, and the need for continuous improvement in gameplay mechanics prompted iterative development and adaptation.

Scalability Challenges: As Axie Infinity gained popularity, the scalability issues on the Ethereum blockchain became evident. High gas fees and slow transaction times posed challenges for players. To address this, Axie Infinity explored layer 2 solutions, such as Ronin, a sidechain built specifically for Axie Infinity, to enhance scalability and reduce transaction costs.

Iterative Development: Axie Infinity's development team actively engages with the community to gather feedback and iteratively improve the game. This commitment to continuous improvement ensures that Axie Infinity remains responsive to player needs, adapts to evolving technological landscapes, and maintains a player-centric approach to game design.

Conclusion: Axie Infinity's Enduring Legacy

In this exploration of Axie Infinity's game design and economics, it becomes clear that Axie Infinity is not just a game but a transformative force in the world of play-to-earn gaming. Its innovative dual-token system, player-driven economy, and community-centric approach have set the standard for subsequent projects. The ripple effects of Axie Infinity extend beyond the virtual realms, influencing how players perceive ownership, collaboration, and economic empowerment in the digital age. The subsequent chapters will unravel the broader impact of Axie Infinity on the first wave of play-to-earn gaming and its role in shaping the future of decentralized economies within the gaming landscape.

Explosive Growth of Axie Infinity in the Philippines and Beyond

Axie Infinity's journey from a blockchain-based game to a socio-economic phenomenon is particularly pronounced in the Philippines. This section explores the unprecedented growth of Axie Infinity in the Philippines and its subsequent impact on global adoption, uncovering the unique factors that propelled Axie to the forefront of play-to-earn gaming.

The Axie Boom in the Philippines: Economic Empowerment Through Gaming

The Philippines became a focal point for Axie Infinity's explosive growth, unlocking economic opportunities for individuals facing financial challenges. This phenomenon is rooted in the confluence of factors that made Axie Infinity not just a game but a lifeline for many in the Philippines.

Economic Landscape in the Philippines: The Philippines has long grappled with economic challenges, including issues of unemployment and limited access to traditional financial systems. Axie Infinity emerged as a beacon of hope, offering a novel avenue for individuals to earn income through gameplay.

Axie as a Source of Livelihood: Earning in Cryptocurrency

Axie Infinity introduced a paradigm shift by allowing players to earn cryptocurrency, particularly Smooth Love Potion (SLP), through gameplay. This proved to be revolutionary in regions where traditional employment opportunities were scarce.

Cryptocurrency as Earned Income: Players in the Philippines found in Axie Infinity not just a game but a source of earned income. The ability to convert in-game efforts into cryptocurrency provided a tangible and valuable resource, especially as SLP gained liquidity and could be traded for other cryptocurrencies or fiat currency.

Beyond Gaming: Economic Inclusion: Axie Infinity became a tool for economic inclusion, bringing individuals who were previously excluded from traditional financial systems into the digital economy. Players, including those with limited educational backgrounds or technical expertise, found a means of participation that transcended traditional barriers.

Community and Social Impact: The Rise of Axie Guilds

The growth of Axie Infinity in the Philippines is inseparable from the sense of community that blossomed around the game. Axie Guilds played a pivotal role in supporting players, fostering collaboration, and amplifying the social impact of Axie Infinity.

Axie Guilds as Support Systems: Guilds within Axie Infinity provided more than just strategic support; they became lifelines for players. Experienced members guided newcomers, offering insights into gameplay mechanics, economic strategies, and navigating the broader Axie community. Guilds created a support system that extended beyond the virtual realms.

Empowering Through Education: Axie Guilds took on an educational role, offering resources and guidance to help players navigate the complexities of blockchain technology, cryptocurrency, and the broader play-to-earn ecosystem. This educational aspect empowered players, enabling them to make informed decisions and actively participate in the digital economy.

Axie Infinity's Ripple Effect: Global Adoption and Cultural Impact

The success of Axie Infinity in the Philippines reverberated globally, triggering a wave of adoption and cultural impact. The Axie phenomenon transcended geographical boundaries, influencing how people perceive the intersection of gaming, blockchain technology, and economic empowerment.

Global Adoption: The success story of Axie Infinity in the Philippines captured the attention of the global gaming community. Players and developers worldwide took note of the potential for blockchain-based games to bring about economic change, leading to increased interest and adoption of play-to-earn models.

Cultural Impact: Redefining Gaming and Income Streams: Axie Infinity's explosive growth contributed to the reshaping of cultural narratives around gaming. It challenged conventional perceptions of gaming as a mere pastime, transforming it into a legitimate and viable source of income. The cultural impact extended beyond gaming communities, permeating discussions around blockchain technology, decentralization, and the future of work.

Challenges Amid Success: Scalability, Accessibility, and Regulation

Axie Infinity's rapid growth brought with it a set of challenges, highlighting the need for ongoing development and adaptation to sustain the momentum. Scalability issues, accessibility concerns, and regulatory considerations emerged as key factors that required attention.

Scalability Challenges: As the user base expanded, scalability issues on the Ethereum blockchain became more pronounced. High gas fees and network congestion prompted the exploration of scalability solutions such as the Ronin sidechain. This challenge underscored the importance of scalable blockchain infrastructure to support the growing demands of play-to-earn ecosystems.

Accessibility Concerns: Bridging the Digital Divide: The success of Axie Infinity in the Philippines shed light on the broader issue of accessibility in play-to-earn gaming. Bridging the digital divide became crucial, necessitating efforts to lower entry barriers, provide educational resources, and improve user interfaces to make blockchain-based games more inclusive.

Regulatory Considerations: Navigating Uncertain Terrain: Axie Infinity's success prompted regulatory scrutiny, requiring developers to navigate uncertain terrain. The intersection of gaming and cryptocurrency raised questions about compliance and oversight. The regulatory landscape remains dynamic, with ongoing discussions about how to strike a balance between fostering innovation and addressing potential risks.

Axie Infinity's Enduring Legacy: Lessons Learned and Future Impact

The explosive growth of Axie Infinity in the Philippines and beyond carries enduring lessons and insights. Axie's impact on economic empowerment, community building, and the redefinition of gaming as a legitimate income stream serves as a foundation for the future of play-to-earn gaming.

Economic Empowerment Through Play: Axie Infinity's success demonstrated the potential for play-to-earn models to empower individuals economically, particularly in regions facing financial challenges. This aspect of Axie's legacy serves as a blueprint for future projects seeking to bring economic inclusion through blockchain-based gaming.

Community Building and Support Systems: The role of Axie Guilds in fostering community, providing support, and enabling educational initiatives stands as a testament to the power of collaborative play-to-earn ecosystems. The community-driven model of Axie Infinity has implications for how future games can leverage social dynamics for success.

Challenges as Catalysts for Improvement: The challenges faced by Axie Infinity, from scalability issues to regulatory considerations, serve as catalysts for ongoing improvement and development. These challenges highlight the need for continuous adaptation, collaboration, and innovation within the play-to-earn gaming space.

Conclusion: Axie Infinity's Extraordinary Chapter in Play-to-Earn History

In examining the explosive growth of Axie Infinity in the Philippines and its global impact, it becomes evident that Axie is not merely a game but a transformative force. Its success has sparked conversations, redefined cultural narratives, and set the stage for a new era where gaming is synonymous with economic empowerment. The subsequent chapters will delve deeper into the broader implications of Axie Infinity's first wave and its role in shaping the evolving landscape of play-to-earn gaming on a global scale.

Other Notable First-Generation Play-to-Earn Games

While Axie Infinity stands as a trailblazer in the play-to-earn gaming space, it is part of a broader movement that saw the emergence of other noteworthy first-generation play-to-earn games. This section explores the landscape of these early pioneers, each contributing to the evolution of decentralized gaming economies and the transformative concept of earning tangible rewards through virtual gameplay.

CryptoKitties: A Pioneering Genesis

Before the rise of Axie Infinity, CryptoKitties marked the beginning of blockchain-based gaming. As explored in a previous chapter, CryptoKitties introduced the concept of digital collectibles, paving the way for the exploration of true ownership and scarcity within the blockchain gaming space.

Unique Features and Cultural Impact: CryptoKitties, with its unique genetic algorithm, introduced players to the idea of breeding and owning virtual cats on the blockchain. The game's cultural impact reached beyond the crypto community, influencing discussions about digital ownership and the potential of blockchain in gaming.

Lessons Learned and Iterative Development: As a first-generation play-to-earn experiment, CryptoKitties provided valuable lessons for subsequent projects. The challenges faced, such as scalability issues on the Ethereum blockchain, informed the iterative development of later games like Axie Infinity.

Decentraland: Virtual Real Estate and User-Generated Content

Decentraland, a virtual world built on the Ethereum blockchain, represents another milestone in the first wave of play-to-earn games. It introduced the concept of virtual real estate ownership and user-generated content within a decentralized metaverse.

Virtual Real Estate and Ownership: Decentraland allowed users to buy, sell, and trade virtual land parcels represented as non-fungible tokens (LAND). The ownership of virtual real estate in Decentraland opened new possibilities for play-to-earn dynamics, as users could monetize their virtual properties and create unique experiences within the metaverse.

User-Generated Content and Creativity: One of Decentraland's strengths lies in its emphasis on user-generated content. Players can create and monetize experiences, games, and assets within the virtual world. This approach fosters a collaborative and creative community, contributing to the overall richness of the Decentraland ecosystem.

Sorare: Fantasy Football on the Blockchain

Sorare brought the play-to-earn model to the world of fantasy sports, specifically focusing on football (soccer). By leveraging blockchain technology, Sorare introduced a novel way for players to earn rewards based on the performance of real-world football players.

Unique Gameplay Mechanics: Sorare allows users to build fantasy football teams using digital player cards that are represented as NFTs. The performance of these players in real-world football matches directly impacts the in-game rewards. This innovative blend of fantasy sports and blockchain technology created a unique play-to-earn experience.

Global Fantasy Football Community: Sorare's global approach to fantasy football encourages the participation of users from around the world. The game's marketplace facilitates the trading of player cards, creating a dynamic ecosystem where the value of virtual assets is influenced by real-world sports events.

Challenges and Lessons from First-Generation Games

While these first-generation play-to-earn games paved the way for the broader adoption of decentralized gaming economies, they also faced challenges that influenced the subsequent evolution of the play-to-earn model.

Scalability and Blockchain Solutions: Scalability issues, often associated with the use of blockchain technology, were a common challenge among first-generation games. The limitations of existing blockchain networks prompted exploration into layer 2 solutions, sidechains, and alternative blockchain architectures to address scalability concerns.

User Onboarding and Education: Educating users about blockchain technology and the intricacies of play-to-earn mechanics presented a significant hurdle. First-generation games learned the importance of user-friendly interfaces, educational resources, and community support to facilitate user onboarding and retention.

The Diverse Tapestry of First-Generation Play-to-Earn Games

Beyond CryptoKitties, Decentraland, and Sorare, the first generation of play-to-earn games included a diverse array of projects, each contributing to the experimentation and exploration of decentralized gaming economies.

Blockchain-Based Card Games: Games like Gods Unchained and Splinterlands explored play-to-earn dynamics within the context of blockchain-based trading card games. These games introduced the concept of owning and trading digital cards with real-world value, creating economic opportunities for players.

Blockchain-Based Collectibles: Projects like Axie Infinity inspired the development of other blockchain-based collectibles, ranging from virtual pets to unique in-game assets.

The concept of true ownership, enabled by blockchain technology, became a common thread among these projects.

Evolution and Impact of First-Generation Games on the Play-to-Earn Ecosystem

The first generation of play-to-earn games, including Axie Infinity, CryptoKitties, Decentraland, Sorare, and others, laid the foundation for a burgeoning ecosystem that continues to evolve. Their impact goes beyond individual projects, shaping the broader narrative of decentralized gaming economies.

Inspiration for Future Projects: These early pioneers inspired a new wave of developers and entrepreneurs to explore the possibilities of play-to-earn models. The success stories and challenges faced by first-generation games provided valuable insights for subsequent projects, fueling innovation and creativity.

Community Building and Engagement: The community-centric approach of first-generation play-to-earn games demonstrated the power of fostering engaged and supportive user communities. This emphasis on community building became a hallmark of successful projects, influencing how developers approached player interaction and collaboration.

Conclusion: A Tapestry of Innovation and Exploration

The first-generation play-to-earn games, each with its unique features and contributions, collectively form a tapestry of innovation and exploration within the decentralized gaming landscape. Their journey, from conceptualizing the idea of true ownership to facing challenges and inspiring future projects, set the stage for the expansive and diverse play-to-earn ecosystem that continues to thrive and evolve. As we move forward in this exploration, the chapters ahead will delve into the challenges faced by early play-to-earn models and the subsequent innovations that propelled the concept to new heights.

Attracting Venture Capital and Mainstream Attention

The success of Axie Infinity transcended the boundaries of gaming communities, capturing the attention of venture capitalists and mainstream audiences alike. This section explores the journey of Axie Infinity as it attracted significant venture capital investments and garnered mainstream attention, marking a pivotal moment in the convergence of gaming, blockchain, and traditional finance.

Venture Capital's Embrace: A Stamp of Legitimacy

Axie Infinity's ascent from a niche blockchain game to a venture capital darling marked a paradigm shift in how investors perceived the intersection of gaming and blockchain technology. The infusion of venture capital not only injected substantial funding into the project but also signaled a broader acknowledgment of the potential of play-to-earn gaming.

Early Investments and Seed Funding: Axie Infinity's journey began with seed funding from early backers who recognized the project's innovative approach to decentralized gaming economies. The initial investments provided the resources needed to develop the game, experiment with economic models, and build a dedicated community.

Venture Capital Influx: As Axie Infinity demonstrated its viability and user adoption, venture capital firms took notice. Significant funding rounds further fueled the development and expansion of the game. The influx of venture capital served as a validation of the play-to-earn model, attracting attention not only within the blockchain and gaming sectors but also from the broader investment community.

Axie's Venture Capital Partnerships: A Strategic Approach

Axie Infinity strategically formed partnerships with prominent venture capital firms, solidifying its position as a leader in the play-to-earn gaming space. These partnerships not only provided financial support but also brought valuable expertise, mentorship, and access to networks that accelerated Axie's growth.

Delphi Digital and Hashed: Venture capital firms like Delphi Digital and Hashed played pivotal roles in Axie Infinity's funding journey. Delphi Digital's expertise in blockchain research and investment strategy complemented Hashed's focus on blockchain projects and community-building. These partnerships went beyond financial backing, contributing to the strategic vision and sustainability of Axie Infinity.

Building Trust and Credibility: Venture capital partnerships brought a level of trust and credibility to Axie Infinity, especially as traditional investors began exploring blockchain opportunities. The involvement of reputable venture capital firms signaled to the broader financial industry that play-to-earn gaming was not just a niche trend but a legitimate and investable sector.

Mainstream Media and Celebrity Endorsements: A Cultural Phenomenon

Axie Infinity's journey from niche blockchain game to a cultural phenomenon was further propelled by mainstream media coverage and endorsements from notable celebrities. The confluence of gaming, blockchain, and mainstream attention created a perfect storm that catapulted Axie into the public consciousness.

Media Coverage and News Outlets: Axie Infinity's unique success story attracted attention from major media outlets. News articles, features, and interviews highlighted the economic empowerment aspects of play-to-earn gaming, showcasing real-world stories of individuals earning income through Axie Infinity. This media coverage played a crucial role in introducing the concept to audiences beyond the gaming and blockchain communities.

Social Media Amplification: The rise of Axie Infinity coincided with the era of social media dominance. Platforms like Twitter, Reddit, and YouTube became breeding grounds for discussions about Axie's impact. Content creators and influencers shared their experiences, strategies, and success stories, contributing to the game's virality and attracting a diverse audience.

Celebrity Endorsements and Influencer Culture

Axie Infinity's journey into mainstream culture was further accelerated by celebrity endorsements and the influence of popular figures. Notable personalities from the entertainment and sports industries openly embraced Axie, adding an additional layer of validation and cultural relevance.

Snoop Dogg and Other Influential Figures: Snoop Dogg, a globally recognized rapper and entrepreneur, publicly endorsed Axie Infinity, bringing a massive following into the world of play-to-earn gaming. His engagement with the game, coupled with endorsements from other influential figures, demonstrated the crossover appeal of Axie Infinity beyond traditional gaming demographics.

Sports Stars and Gaming Culture: The fusion of sports, gaming, and blockchain found a nexus in Axie Infinity. Athletes and sports stars, recognizing the potential for economic empowerment and community engagement, actively participated in and endorsed Axie Infinity. This intersection of gaming and sports culture broadened the game's reach and solidified its status as a cultural phenomenon.

Axie in the Headlines: Navigating Challenges and Embracing Success

As Axie Infinity attracted venture capital and mainstream attention, it also faced challenges and controversies that came with increased visibility. From navigating scalability issues to addressing concerns about the sustainability of play-to-earn models, Axie's journey was not without hurdles.

Scalability and Ronin Sidechain: The surge in popularity brought scalability challenges on the Ethereum blockchain. To address this, Axie Infinity implemented the Ronin sidechain, a layer 2 solution designed specifically for the game. The transition to Ronin aimed to enhance scalability, reduce transaction costs, and improve overall user experience.

Sustainability and Economic Models: As Axie Infinity scaled, questions arose about the sustainability of its play-to-earn model. The team continually iterated on economic models, introducing features like staking and governance to balance the in-game economy. These adjustments reflected Axie's commitment to addressing challenges and ensuring the long-term viability of its ecosystem.

The Broader Impact: Redefining Gaming and Economic Participation

The confluence of venture capital investments, mainstream media attention, and celebrity endorsements contributed to Axie Infinity's broader impact on the perception of gaming and economic participation. Axie's success became a case study for how blockchain technology could redefine traditional industries.

Blockchain Gaming as an Investable Sector: Axie Infinity's success opened the floodgates for venture capital interest in blockchain gaming. The game served as a proof of concept for the viability of play-to-earn models, encouraging investors to explore opportunities within the broader blockchain gaming sector.

Cultural Shift in Gaming: Axie Infinity's cultural impact extended beyond its play-to-earn mechanics. It sparked a cultural shift in how gaming is perceived, transforming it from a leisure activity to a legitimate avenue for economic empowerment. The concept of true ownership and earning real-world value through virtual gameplay became embedded in the cultural narrative surrounding gaming.

Conclusion: Axie Infinity's Dual Triumph in Finance and Pop Culture

As Axie Infinity attracted venture capital and mainstream attention, it achieved a dual triumph. On one front, it secured financial backing and partnerships that bolstered its development and sustainability. Simultaneously, Axie's cultural phenomenon status transcended gaming communities, reaching mainstream audiences and reshaping perceptions of gaming, blockchain, and economic participation. The subsequent chapters will delve deeper into the challenges faced by Axie Infinity, its ongoing evolution, and the lessons learned that continue to shape the play-to-earn gaming landscape.

Limitations and Criticisms of Early Play-to-Earn Models

While the first wave of play-to-earn gaming, led by Axie Infinity, brought about transformative possibilities, it also faced its share of limitations and criticisms. This section explores the challenges and criticisms that early play-to-earn models encountered, shedding light on the complexities and nuances that emerged as these pioneering projects sought to redefine the gaming landscape.

1. Flawed Incentives and Pyramid Scheme Dynamics:

In the early stages of play-to-earn gaming, some projects faced criticism for exhibiting characteristics reminiscent of pyramid schemes. The incentive structures, particularly those heavily reliant on new player recruitment, raised concerns about the sustainability and fairness of the models.

Incentives Focused on Recruitment: Certain play-to-earn projects incentivized players to recruit new participants as a primary means of earning rewards. While this initially contributed to rapid user acquisition, it also raised ethical questions about the long-term viability and fairness of such models.

Pyramid Scheme Dynamics: The reliance on recruitment-driven incentives led to pyramid-like dynamics, where early adopters benefited significantly from the efforts of those they recruited. As the player base expanded, sustaining the promised rewards became challenging, resulting in dissatisfaction and criticism from participants.

Impact on Long-Term Sustainability: The pyramid scheme dynamics inherent in some early play-to-earn models jeopardized their long-term sustainability. As the player base grew, maintaining the promised rewards for all participants became increasingly challenging, leading to issues of economic imbalance and dissatisfaction among players.

2. Lack of Engaging Gameplay Beyond Basic Grinding:

A recurring criticism of early play-to-earn models was the perceived lack of engaging and enjoyable gameplay experiences. Some projects prioritized economic incentives over the development of compelling game mechanics, resulting in gameplay that felt repetitive and uninspiring.

Emphasis on Economic Mechanics: In the pursuit of creating robust economic models, some play-to-earn projects placed disproportionate emphasis on incentivizing grinding and repetitive tasks to earn rewards. This approach, while effective in driving initial adoption, failed to sustain long-term player engagement.

User Experience and Gameplay Quality: The lack of engaging gameplay experiences raised questions about the long-term viability of play-to-earn models. Players expressed concerns about the sustainability of projects that prioritized economic incentives over the quality of the gaming experience.

Balancing Economics and Gameplay: Early play-to-earn models faced the challenge of striking a balance between economic incentives and engaging gameplay. The criticism prompted developers to reassess their priorities, leading to a shift toward creating games that not only rewarded players economically but also provided enjoyable and immersive experiences.

3. Market Declines and Loss of Interest Among Early Adopters:

The early play-to-earn landscape witnessed fluctuations in market dynamics, with periods of rapid growth followed by declines in user activity. This volatility contributed to concerns about the long-term viability of play-to-earn models and the potential for market saturation.

Market Dynamics and Token Valuations: The value of in-game tokens and assets in play-to-earn ecosystems often experienced fluctuations based on market sentiment and external factors. Rapid increases in token values attracted attention, but subsequent declines led to uncertainties about the sustainability of economic models.

Loss of Interest Among Early Adopters: As market dynamics fluctuated, some early adopters experienced a decline in interest and participation. The shift in focus from play-to-earn dynamics to economic speculation raised questions about the fundamental value and utility of in-game assets.

Lessons Learned: Economic Stability and User Retention: The market declines prompted developers to reevaluate their economic models, emphasizing the importance of stability and user retention. Projects began exploring mechanisms to mitigate market volatility and ensure a more sustainable and enjoyable user experience.

4. Questions About Longevity and Limiting Factors:

The early success of play-to-earn models sparked discussions about their long-term viability and the factors that could limit their widespread adoption. Questions arose regarding the potential barriers that could impede the growth and sustainability of play-to-earn ecosystems.

Longevity Beyond Hype: The initial hype surrounding play-to-earn gaming raised questions about the longevity of the model beyond the excitement of early adoption. Skepticism emerged regarding whether play-to-earn could sustain interest and economic viability over the long term.

Barriers to Entry and Accessibility: Concerns were raised about potential barriers to entry that could limit the accessibility of play-to-earn models. Factors such as technical complexity, the need for cryptocurrency knowledge, and high entry costs were identified as potential limiting factors.

Regulatory Uncertainties: The evolving regulatory landscape surrounding blockchain and gaming introduced uncertainties that could impact the long-term viability of play-to-earn models. Developers and investors grappled with navigating regulatory challenges and ensuring compliance with emerging frameworks.

5. Educational Gaps and Onboarding Challenges:

The intersection of blockchain technology and gaming introduced a learning curve for users unfamiliar with cryptocurrency concepts. Educational gaps and onboarding challenges emerged as significant hurdles in the widespread adoption of play-to-earn models.

Cryptocurrency Literacy and Education: Play-to-earn models required users to navigate cryptocurrency wallets, exchanges, and blockchain transactions. The lack of widespread cryptocurrency literacy posed challenges for onboarding new users and ensuring a seamless experience within play-to-earn ecosystems.

Community Support and Tutorials: Recognizing the importance of education, some projects began investing in community support initiatives and tutorials to bridge the educational gap. User-friendly guides, video tutorials, and community-driven initiatives aimed to enhance the onboarding experience for players, addressing one of the early challenges.

6. Ethical Concerns and Potential Exploitation:

The success of play-to-earn models brought attention to ethical considerations and concerns about potential exploitation within gaming ecosystems. Discussions emerged around player rights, fair compensation, and the responsibilities of developers in fostering healthy gaming environments.

Exploitative Dynamics and Player Rights: Critics raised concerns about exploitative dynamics, particularly in models heavily reliant on recruitment and new player onboarding. Questions were raised about the ethical implications of incentivizing player recruitment and the potential for exploitation within gaming communities.

Player Protections and Governance: The ethical considerations prompted discussions about the need for player protections and governance mechanisms within play-to-earn ecosystems. Projects began exploring ways to empower players, implement fair economic models, and establish transparent governance structures to address ethical concerns.

Conclusion: Navigating Challenges Toward Evolution

The limitations and criticisms faced by early play-to-earn models, including Axie Infinity, served as catalysts for evolution and improvement. Developers, investors, and communities engaged in continuous dialogue, adapting models to address challenges, enhance user experiences, and lay the groundwork for the future chapters of play-to-earn gaming. The subsequent sections will delve into the iterative development and innovations that emerged as play-to-earn models navigated these early challenges, shaping the trajectory of the entire ecosystem.

Chapter 3 - Challenges and Growing Pains
Collapses of Major Projects Like Uplandme Due to Flawed Incentives

In the dynamic landscape of play-to-earn gaming, the journey is not always paved with success stories. Some major projects, such as Uplandme, faced significant challenges that led to their eventual collapse. This section explores the collapse of Uplandme and the role that flawed incentives played in its downfall.

Uplandme: An Ambitious Vision Unraveled

Uplandme entered the play-to-earn gaming scene with an ambitious vision—to create a virtual metaverse where players could buy, sell, and trade virtual properties represented as non-fungible tokens (NFTs) on the blockchain. The project aimed to combine elements of virtual real estate ownership, social interaction, and economic opportunities within a decentralized gaming environment.

1. Flawed Incentives and Economic Imbalance

One of the critical factors contributing to Uplandme's collapse was the presence of flawed incentives within its economic model. The platform incentivized users to invest heavily in virtual properties with the promise of lucrative returns. However, these incentives proved to be unsustainable and led to economic imbalances within the Uplandme ecosystem.

Investment-Driven Gameplay: Uplandme's economic model emphasized the speculative aspect of virtual real estate, encouraging players to view in-game properties as investments rather than interactive gameplay elements. This skewed focus on investment-driven gameplay created an environment where the primary motivation for participation became financial gain rather than immersive gaming experiences.

Economic Imbalance and Inequality: The flawed incentives within Uplandme's model resulted in economic imbalances, with a concentration of wealth and virtual assets among a small subset of players. This inequality not only impacted the overall user experience but also raised ethical concerns about the fairness and inclusivity of the play-to-earn ecosystem.

2. Lack of Sustainable Gameplay Dynamics

Another contributing factor to Uplandme's collapse was the lack of sustainable gameplay dynamics. The platform struggled to offer engaging and enduring gameplay experiences beyond the initial excitement of virtual property acquisition.

Limited Gameplay Beyond Property Trading: Uplandme primarily revolved around the trading of virtual properties, and the gameplay mechanics were limited in scope. The lack of diverse and compelling gameplay activities contributed to user boredom and disengagement over time, eroding the platform's long-term viability.

Dependence on Economic Speculation: The absence of sustainable gameplay dynamics led to a heavy reliance on economic speculation. As users faced diminishing returns from property trading, the platform's appeal waned, and the absence of diversified gameplay mechanics became a critical limiting factor in retaining an active player base.

3. Pyramid Scheme Dynamics and User Recruitment

Uplandme, like some other projects of its time, exhibited elements of pyramid scheme dynamics, relying heavily on user recruitment as a primary means of economic growth. The emphasis on recruiting new players to sustain the economic model created inherent challenges and vulnerabilities.

Recruitment as a Primary Driver: Uplandme's economic model incentivized existing players to recruit new participants into the ecosystem, promising rewards based on the recruitment efforts. This recruitment-centric approach became a primary driver of economic growth but introduced elements of instability and unsustainability.

Challenges of Sustaining Recruitment Levels: Pyramid scheme dynamics, with a focus on recruitment, faced challenges in sustaining high levels of user acquisition. As the player base grew, maintaining the recruitment momentum became increasingly difficult, leading to a collapse in the model's ability to deliver on promised rewards.

4. Regulatory Scrutiny and Compliance Challenges

Uplandme, like many projects in the decentralized gaming space, encountered regulatory scrutiny and compliance challenges. The evolving regulatory landscape presented uncertainties that impacted the project's ability to operate within legal frameworks.

Regulatory Concerns in the Play-to-Earn Space: The intersection of gaming and blockchain technology attracted attention from regulatory bodies seeking to understand and regulate decentralized finance (DeFi) and play-to-earn models. Uplandme, along with other projects, faced challenges in navigating regulatory uncertainties and adapting to emerging frameworks.

Impact on User Trust and Confidence: The regulatory challenges not only posed legal hurdles for Uplandme but also had a psychological impact on user trust and confidence. Concerns about the platform's compliance with regulations raised questions about the security and legitimacy of in-game assets and financial transactions.

5. Lessons Learned from Uplandme's Collapse

The collapse of Uplandme serves as a valuable case study in understanding the potential pitfalls and challenges faced by play-to-earn projects. Several lessons emerged from Uplandme's downfall that have since influenced the development and evolution of subsequent projects in the decentralized gaming space.

Importance of Diversified Gameplay: Uplandme's collapse highlighted the significance of offering diversified and sustainable gameplay experiences. Play-to-earn projects learned from this experience, emphasizing the need for engaging activities beyond economic speculation to retain user interest and ensure long-term success.

Ethical Economic Models and Incentives: The flawed incentives within Uplandme's economic model underscored the importance of designing ethical play-to-earn models. Projects that followed incorporated lessons about fair economic incentives, avoiding exploitative dynamics, and prioritizing user experience over speculative gain.

Balancing Economic Growth and Regulatory Compliance: Uplandme's regulatory challenges emphasized the importance of balancing economic growth with compliance. Play-to-earn projects post-Uplandme have sought to proactively address regulatory considerations, fostering a more secure and legally compliant environment for users.

Conclusion: Uplandme's Legacy and the Evolution of Play-to-Earn

The collapse of Uplandme stands as a cautionary tale in the narrative of play-to-earn gaming. While the project faced significant challenges and ultimately ceased operations, the lessons learned from Uplandme's downfall have contributed to the ongoing evolution of play-to-earn models. Subsequent chapters will delve into how the challenges faced by Uplandme influenced the maturation of play-to-earn gaming, shaping the landscape for future projects and innovations.

Lack of Fun and Engaging Gameplay Beyond Basic Grinding

In the early stages of play-to-earn gaming, one of the prevalent challenges faced by projects was the perceived lack of fun and engaging gameplay experiences beyond basic grinding. While the promise of earning real-world value through in-game activities attracted initial attention, sustaining player interest required a careful balance between economic incentives and immersive gameplay. This section explores the dynamics of gameplay in the play-to-earn landscape and the evolving strategies employed to address the challenge of keeping players entertained.

1. The Initial Appeal of Economic Incentives

Play-to-earn gaming emerged as a revolutionary concept, challenging traditional gaming paradigms by introducing the potential for players to earn tangible rewards. In the early days, the economic incentives took center stage, capturing the imagination of gamers who saw an opportunity to turn their passion into a source of income.

Grinding for Rewards: The initial appeal often revolved around the concept of grinding – performing in-game tasks and activities to earn rewards. Players embraced the idea of putting in time and effort to accumulate virtual assets that held real-world value, creating a novel intersection of gaming and financial incentives.

Early Success Stories: Projects that embraced the play-to-earn model experienced early success, with players flocking to platforms where the promise of economic rewards was most pronounced. The allure of financial gains contributed to rapid user adoption but also set the stage for the subsequent challenge of maintaining player engagement.

2. The Pitfall of Repetitive Gameplay Mechanics

As the play-to-earn model gained traction, some projects fell into the pitfall of relying heavily on repetitive gameplay mechanics centered around basic grinding. The initial excitement of earning rewards through in-game activities began to wane as players encountered monotonous and uninspiring gameplay experiences.

Monotony of Grinding: Many play-to-earn games struggled with a lack of diversity in gameplay activities. Players found themselves engaged in repetitive tasks that felt more like work than play, leading to a decline in overall enjoyment and enthusiasm for the gaming experience.

Impact on Player Retention: The lack of engaging gameplay mechanics had a direct impact on player retention. Users, drawn in by the promise of economic incentives, started disengaging when the grind became the primary focus, highlighting the need for projects to evolve beyond basic repetitive tasks.

3. Evolving Strategies: From Grinding to Engaging Gameplay

Recognizing the challenge posed by a lack of engaging gameplay, play-to-earn projects started to shift their strategies, placing a renewed emphasis on creating immersive and enjoyable gaming experiences. This marked a crucial turning point in the evolution of play-to-earn gaming.

Game Design Innovation: Developers began investing in innovative game design, introducing new mechanics and features that went beyond the traditional grind. The goal was to make the gameplay itself a rewarding and enjoyable experience, ensuring that players found intrinsic value in the activities they were engaged in.

Expanding Game Genres: To address the monotony associated with grinding, play-to-earn projects diversified their offerings by exploring a broader range of game genres. This expansion allowed developers to tap into different player preferences, offering experiences that appealed to a more extensive and diverse audience.

4. True Ownership of Assets and NFT Integration

One of the key strategies employed to enhance gameplay experiences was the integration of non-fungible tokens (NFTs) and the concept of true ownership of in-game assets. This approach aimed to add a layer of authenticity and value to virtual items, creating a sense of ownership that transcended the digital realm.

NFTs and In-Game Assets: Projects recognized that players would find greater satisfaction in their in-game achievements if those achievements were represented as NFTs. This not only added a layer of rarity and uniqueness to virtual items but also allowed players to truly own and trade their assets, contributing to a more immersive and fulfilling gaming experience.

Player-Driven Economies: The integration of NFTs not only empowered players with true ownership but also facilitated player-driven economies. In-game assets became tradable commodities with real-world value, encouraging players to actively participate in the virtual marketplace and contribute to the overall dynamism of the game's ecosystem.

5. Creating Vibrant Virtual Worlds and Communities

Acknowledging the importance of player engagement beyond economic incentives, projects focused on creating vibrant virtual worlds and fostering active communities. The aim was to make the gaming environment more than just a backdrop for grinding, turning it into a social and interactive space.

Immersive Environments: Developers invested in building immersive virtual worlds with rich storytelling, dynamic environments, and interactive elements. This shift aimed to provide players with a sense of exploration and discovery, moving away from the narrow focus on grinding and expanding the dimensions of the gaming experience.

Community Interaction and Events: Active community engagement became a priority, with projects organizing events, tournaments, and collaborative activities. This not only added layers of excitement to the gaming experience but also forged stronger connections among players, fostering a sense of belonging to a larger, dynamic community.

6. Balancing Playability and Earnings Potential

A critical aspect of addressing the lack of engaging gameplay was finding the right balance between playability and earnings potential. Play-to-earn projects aimed to create environments where players could enjoy the gameplay while still having opportunities to earn meaningful rewards.

Reward Structures Aligned with Gameplay: Developers restructured reward systems to align more closely with enjoyable gameplay. Instead of solely tying rewards to repetitive tasks, projects began rewarding players for skillful achievements, strategic decision-making, and meaningful contributions to the virtual world.

Skill-Based Challenges and Achievements: To inject elements of skill and strategy, play-to-earn games introduced skill-based challenges and achievements. These features not only rewarded players for mastering the game but also elevated the overall level of competition, making the gaming experience more dynamic and rewarding.

7. The Ongoing Evolution: Lessons and Iterations

The efforts to address the lack of engaging gameplay beyond basic grinding have marked a continuous evolution in play-to-earn gaming. As projects learn from early challenges, player feedback, and market dynamics, they iterate on their models to enhance the overall gaming experience.

User Feedback and Iterative Development: Projects actively seek and incorporate user feedback to inform iterative development. This collaborative approach allows developers to identify pain points, understand player preferences, and implement changes that resonate with the community, contributing to an ongoing cycle of improvement.

Emerging Trends and Innovations: The evolving landscape of play-to-earn gaming sees the emergence of new trends and innovations. From the integration of virtual reality (VR) and augmented reality (AR) to the exploration of blockchain interoperability, projects continue to push boundaries, introducing features that redefine what is possible in the realm of gaming.

Conclusion: A Balanced Future for Play-to-Earn Gaming

The challenge of addressing the lack of fun and engaging gameplay beyond basic grinding has spurred a transformative journey for play-to-earn gaming. As projects strike a balance between economic incentives and immersive gameplay, the future promises a more holistic and enjoyable experience for players. The subsequent chapters will delve into the broader implications of these innovations, exploring the impact on player ecosystems, project sustainability, and the maturation of play-to-earn economies.

Pyramid Scheme Dynamics and Reliance on New Players

In the evolving landscape of play-to-earn gaming, the challenge of pyramid scheme dynamics and the reliance on new players has been a significant hurdle for some projects. This section delves into the intricacies of how certain play-to-earn models unintentionally adopted elements reminiscent of pyramid schemes, exploring the consequences of such dynamics and the subsequent efforts to create more sustainable and equitable ecosystems.

1. Unraveling the Pyramid Scheme Dynamics

As play-to-earn gaming gained popularity, some projects found themselves unintentionally entangled in pyramid scheme dynamics. The allure of quick economic gains and the reliance on new player recruitment as a primary driver for success created a system that echoed elements of pyramid schemes.

Incentivizing Recruitment as a Priority: In the pursuit of rapid growth, certain play-to-earn projects incentivized existing players to recruit new participants aggressively. The promise of additional rewards for bringing in new players became a central component of the economic model, inadvertently introducing pyramid-like structures.

Rewards Tied to Recruitment Levels: Players were often rewarded based on the recruitment levels they achieved, creating a system where early adopters benefited significantly from the efforts of those they recruited. This structure, while initially fueling growth, raised ethical questions about the sustainability and fairness of the models.

2. Unsustainability and Economic Imbalance

The reliance on new player recruitment, akin to pyramid schemes, led to inherent challenges in sustaining the economic balance within play-to-earn ecosystems. As the player base expanded, maintaining the promised rewards for all participants became increasingly difficult, resulting in economic imbalances.

Challenges in Sustaining Recruitment Momentum: Pyramid scheme dynamics faced challenges in sustaining high levels of user acquisition. As the player base grew, maintaining the recruitment momentum became increasingly difficult, leading to a collapse in the model's ability to deliver on promised rewards.

Concentration of Wealth and Assets: The unintended consequences of pyramid-like structures included a concentration of wealth and virtual assets among a small subset of players. Economic imbalances created inequalities within the ecosystem, diminishing the overall fairness and inclusivity of the play-to-earn model.

3. Impact on Long-Term Sustainability

Pyramid scheme dynamics introduced fragility into the long-term sustainability of play-to-earn models. The focus on recruitment-driven growth posed challenges in maintaining economic stability, leading to uncertainties about the viability and durability of the play-to-earn ecosystem.

Erosion of Trust and Community Confidence: As projects faced difficulties in sustaining the promised rewards, player trust and confidence eroded. Participants who joined with the expectation of ongoing economic benefits began to question the legitimacy and sustainability of the play-to-earn model, impacting the overall community sentiment.

Lessons Learned: Shifting Toward Equitable Models: The challenges posed by pyramid scheme dynamics prompted developers and communities to reflect on the importance of creating equitable and sustainable play-to-earn models. Lessons learned from the unsustainability of recruitment-centric growth influenced subsequent iterations, emphasizing fairness and long-term viability.

4. Evolving Strategies: Beyond Recruitment-Centric Models

Acknowledging the pitfalls of recruitment-centric models, play-to-earn projects initiated strategic shifts to move beyond pyramid scheme dynamics. These shifts aimed to foster a more inclusive and sustainable ecosystem, steering away from overreliance on new player recruitment.

Focus on User Engagement and Retention: Projects began prioritizing user engagement and retention as key indicators of success. Rather than relying solely on recruitment as a growth metric, the emphasis shifted to creating compelling gameplay experiences that retained existing players and attracted new participants organically.

Community Building and Collaboration: To break free from pyramid scheme dynamics, play-to-earn models embraced community-building strategies. Projects actively sought to create collaborative and supportive player communities, fostering an environment where users felt valued beyond their recruitment potential.

5. Implementing Fair Distribution Mechanisms

To address economic imbalances arising from pyramid-like structures, play-to-earn projects explored fair distribution mechanisms that ensured a more even distribution of rewards among participants. This marked a departure from models heavily skewed towards early adopters.

Decentralized Governance and Decision-Making: Projects embraced decentralized governance structures that empowered the community to participate in decision-making processes. This shift aimed to distribute decision-making authority and economic benefits more equitably, reducing the concentration of power and rewards within a select group.

Dynamic Reward Models: To mitigate economic imbalances, dynamic reward models were introduced. These models adjusted rewards based on various factors such as user contributions, gameplay achievements, and overall ecosystem health, fostering a more meritocratic distribution of incentives.

6.   Educational   Initiatives   and   Transparent Communication

Addressing pyramid scheme dynamics required not only changes in economic models but also a commitment to transparent communication and educational initiatives. Play-to-earn projects recognized the importance of empowering users with information to make informed decisions.

Transparent Communication about Risks: Projects actively communicated the risks associated with play-to-earn models, especially those that relied heavily on recruitment. Transparency about the potential challenges and uncertainties allowed users to make informed choices and set realistic expectations.

Educational   Initiatives   for   User   Empowerment: Educational initiatives became integral to the ecosystem's evolution. Projects invested in resources, tutorials, and guides that educated users about the mechanics of play-to-earn gaming, blockchain technology, and the potential risks associated with specific economic models.

7. Regulatory Considerations and Compliance

The unintentional adoption of pyramid scheme dynamics drew attention to the need for regulatory considerations within the play-to-earn space. Developers and stakeholders engaged with regulatory bodies to ensure compliance with emerging frameworks.

Navigating Regulatory Uncertainties: Regulatory uncertainties presented challenges for play-to-earn projects. The evolving legal landscape prompted a proactive approach to compliance, with projects actively seeking to navigate regulatory uncertainties and establish frameworks that ensured adherence to legal standards.

Building Trust through Compliance: Compliance with regulatory standards became a means of building trust within the play-to-earn community. Projects that embraced regulatory considerations demonstrated a commitment to responsible and ethical practices, fostering a sense of security among participants.

8. Community-Led Initiatives for Fairness and Accountability

Community-led initiatives played a crucial role in fostering fairness and accountability within play-to-earn ecosystems. Participants themselves became advocates for equitable practices, influencing the evolution of projects toward more sustainable and community-centric models.

Emergence of Player Advocacy Groups: Player advocacy groups and communities emerged to champion fairness and accountability. These groups actively engaged with projects, providing feedback, holding discussions, and advocating for changes that prioritized the interests of the broader community.

Collaborative Decision-Making: Projects increasingly embraced collaborative decision-making, involving the community in governance structures and decision processes. This shift empowered players to voice concerns, propose changes, and actively contribute to the shaping of the play-to-earn landscape.

Conclusion: Navigating the Pyramid Scheme Challenge

The challenges posed by pyramid scheme dynamics and the reliance on new players prompted a transformative journey within the play-to-earn gaming space. Through a combination of strategic shifts, educational initiatives, regulatory considerations, and community-led efforts, projects navigated these challenges, paving the way for a more equitable and sustainable future. The subsequent chapters will explore the ongoing evolution of play-to-earn gaming, examining the broader impacts on user ecosystems, regulatory landscapes, and the maturation of play-to-earn economies.

Market Declines and Loss of Interest Among Early Adopters

In the dynamic realm of play-to-earn gaming, the challenge of market declines and the subsequent loss of interest among early adopters has been a significant factor shaping the evolution of these ecosystems. This section delves into the multifaceted aspects of market dynamics, exploring the causes and consequences of declines, and examining how play-to-earn projects have navigated these challenges to sustain and revitalize interest among their earliest supporters.

1. The Initial Hype and Early Adoption Surge

As play-to-earn gaming burst onto the scene, it brought with it a wave of excitement and anticipation. Early adopters, drawn by the promise of earning real-world value through in-game activities, flocked to these projects, contributing to a surge in user adoption and market activity.

Economic Potential Fuels Early Enthusiasm: The initial wave of early adopters was often driven by the economic potential of play-to-earn models. The prospect of converting time and skill invested in games into tangible rewards resonated strongly with users, leading to an enthusiastic embrace of these novel gaming ecosystems.

Hype-Driven Growth and Speculation: Hype around play-to-earn projects contributed to rapid growth and speculation. Prices of in-game assets and associated tokens soared, creating an environment where early adopters saw substantial returns on their initial investments, further fueling the enthusiasm within the community.

2. Market Dynamics: Peaks and Valleys

While the early stages saw unprecedented growth, the nascent play-to-earn market was not immune to the cyclical nature of cryptocurrency markets. Market dynamics, influenced by various external factors, experienced peaks followed by inevitable declines, impacting the overall sentiment and engagement of early adopters.

Volatility and External Factors: Cryptocurrency markets, including those associated with play-to-earn tokens, are known for their inherent volatility. External factors such as regulatory developments, macroeconomic trends, and technological advancements can trigger fluctuations, leading to periods of market decline.

Speculative Nature and Corrections: The speculative nature of play-to-earn tokens, coupled with market corrections, meant that the valuations experienced rapid shifts. As prices corrected from inflated levels, early adopters faced the reality of market volatility, impacting the perceived value of their in-game assets.

3. Consequences of Market Declines on Player Sentiment

Market declines have far-reaching consequences on player sentiment, especially among early adopters who were instrumental in the initial success of play-to-earn projects. The psychological and economic impact of witnessing the value of their assets decrease can contribute to a loss of interest and engagement.

Psychological Impact: The psychological impact of market declines cannot be understated. Early adopters, who may have entered the play-to-earn ecosystem with high expectations, face challenges in reconciling the initial hype with the realities of market fluctuations. This disillusionment can lead to a decline in overall sentiment.

Economic Losses and Asset Devaluation: As market values decline, early adopters may experience economic losses and witness the devaluation of their in-game assets. The perceived loss of value can create a sense of disappointment, prompting some participants to disengage from the ecosystem or reconsider their level of involvement.

4. Navigating Challenges: Strategies Employed by Projects

In response to market declines and the potential loss of interest among early adopters, play-to-earn projects have implemented strategic measures to navigate these challenges. These strategies aim to restore confidence, rekindle engagement, and fortify the long-term sustainability of the gaming ecosystems.

Communication and Transparency: Transparent communication is paramount during periods of market decline. Projects that openly communicate about market dynamics, address concerns, and provide realistic expectations can build trust among their early adopters, fostering a sense of community resilience.

Innovative Economic Models: To mitigate the impact of market fluctuations, some projects have explored innovative economic models. This includes mechanisms such as staking, yield farming, and dynamic tokenomics designed to add stability and utility to the in-game tokens, reducing reliance on speculative value alone.

5. The Role of Community Engagement and Incentives

Recognizing the pivotal role of early adopters, play-to-earn projects have increasingly focused on community engagement strategies and tailored incentives to maintain interest during market downturns.

Community-Led Initiatives: Community engagement goes beyond economic considerations. Projects that encourage community-led initiatives, such as tournaments, events, and collaborative activities, create a sense of belonging that extends beyond the economic aspects, fostering a resilient and committed user base.

Tailored Incentives and Rewards: In response to market challenges, projects have implemented tailored incentives and reward structures. These incentives could include exclusive in-game items, limited-edition NFTs, or participation in governance decisions, providing early adopters with additional motivations beyond token value.

6. Lessons Learned: Adapting to Market Realities

The challenges posed by market declines and the subsequent loss of interest among early adopters have imparted valuable lessons to play-to-earn projects. Adaptability, resilience, and a commitment to long-term goals have become integral components of successful strategies.

Balancing Short-Term Gains and Long-Term Vision: Projects have learned the importance of balancing short-term market dynamics with a steadfast commitment to long-term visions. While market declines may present immediate challenges, maintaining focus on the project's underlying goals contributes to sustained community trust.

Iterative Development and Continuous Improvement: The iterative nature of play-to-earn projects allows for continuous improvement. Learning from market downturns, projects iteratively develop and enhance their models, addressing the concerns of early adopters, and adapting to the evolving dynamics of the gaming and crypto markets.

7. Regulatory Considerations and Risk Mitigation

Market declines also underscore the importance of regulatory considerations and risk mitigation strategies. The play-to-earn space, situated at the intersection of gaming and blockchain, necessitates proactive measures to navigate potential regulatory challenges and enhance overall ecosystem resilience.

Engaging with Regulatory Authorities: Projects that proactively engage with regulatory authorities and adhere to emerging frameworks demonstrate a commitment to long-term sustainability. Regulatory compliance builds confidence among early adopters and provides a foundation for the project's continued growth.

Risk Mitigation and Contingency Planning: In anticipation of market uncertainties, play-to-earn projects have incorporated risk mitigation and contingency planning into their strategies. This includes measures such as diversification of economic models, liquidity management, and scenario planning to cushion the impact of adverse market conditions.

8. The Ongoing Evolution: Maturing Through Challenges

While market declines and the potential loss of interest among early adopters present formidable challenges, they are integral to the ongoing evolution and maturation of play-to-earn gaming. By learning from experiences, implementing strategic adaptations, and fostering a resilient community, projects navigate these challenges, laying the groundwork for a more robust and sustainable future.

Conclusion: A Resilient Future for Play-to-Earn Gaming

The journey through market declines and the associated loss of interest among early adopters has been a transformative chapter for play-to-earn gaming. As projects navigate the complexities of market dynamics, they evolve, adapt, and fortify their foundations, ensuring a resilient future that extends beyond the peaks and valleys of the cryptocurrency landscape. The subsequent chapters will explore further dimensions of challenges, growth, and innovation within the play-to-earn ecosystem.

Questions about Longevity and Limiting Factors

In the landscape of play-to-earn gaming, questions about longevity and the identification of limiting factors have emerged as pivotal considerations for the sustained growth and viability of these ecosystems. This section delves into the multifaceted aspects of these questions, exploring the potential challenges that may impact the long-term success of play-to-earn projects and how the industry is addressing these concerns to ensure a robust and enduring future.

1. The Allure of Longevity: A Vital Consideration

As play-to-earn gaming projects continue to gain traction, the notion of longevity becomes a focal point. The allure of sustaining a project beyond initial successes involves navigating various challenges and proactively addressing potential limiting factors to ensure lasting relevance.

Understanding Longevity in Play-to-Earn: Longevity in play-to-earn gaming extends beyond short-term gains. It encompasses the ability of a project to maintain player interest, economic sustainability, and community engagement over an extended period. The identification of factors influencing longevity is crucial for developers and stakeholders.

Striking a Balance: Balancing short-term goals with a long-term vision is central to ensuring the longevity of play-to-earn projects. Striking this balance involves addressing immediate challenges while simultaneously making strategic decisions that contribute to sustained growth and resilience.

2. Exploring Potential Limiting Factors

To comprehend the questions surrounding longevity, it's imperative to explore potential limiting factors that may hinder the continuous growth and evolution of play-to-earn gaming. Identifying these factors is a proactive step toward developing strategies to mitigate their impact.

Economic Sustainability: One of the primary limiting factors is the economic sustainability of play-to-earn models. Projects heavily reliant on economic incentives may face challenges in maintaining a balance between rewards for players and the overall health of the in-game economy.

Regulatory Uncertainties: The evolving regulatory landscape poses another potential limiting factor. Play-to-earn projects operate at the intersection of gaming and blockchain, necessitating a nuanced approach to compliance. Regulatory uncertainties can create challenges that may impact the long-term viability of these ecosystems.

3. Economic Sustainability and Player Incentives

Addressing questions about longevity involves a deep dive into the economic sustainability of play-to-earn models and the strategies implemented to ensure continued player incentives. The evolving nature of economic systems within these projects requires a dynamic approach to sustain player engagement.

Balancing Incentives and Ecosystem Health: Maintaining a balance between providing lucrative incentives for players and safeguarding the overall health of the ecosystem is a delicate challenge. Play-to-earn projects are exploring innovative economic models that align incentives with sustainable growth, reducing the risk of economic imbalances.

Iterative Tokenomics and Economic Models: An iterative approach to tokenomics and economic models is becoming a hallmark of projects seeking longevity. Continuous refinement based on user feedback, market dynamics, and lessons learned from challenges contributes to the development of robust and adaptive economic systems.

4. The Regulatory Landscape: Navigating Uncertainties

The regulatory landscape presents a significant factor influencing the longevity of play-to-earn projects. As governments worldwide grapple with the classification and oversight of blockchain-based assets, play-to-earn initiatives must proactively engage with regulatory authorities.

Proactive Engagement and Compliance: Proactive engagement with regulatory authorities is critical for play-to-earn projects. Compliance with emerging regulatory frameworks not only mitigates legal risks but also fosters an environment of trust and legitimacy, key elements for long-term success.

Global Standards and Local Adaptations: Navigating the regulatory landscape involves considering both global standards and local adaptations. Play-to-earn projects are finding ways to adhere to overarching regulatory principles while respecting the specific legal nuances of individual jurisdictions, ensuring a resilient and adaptable approach.

5. Technological Advancements and Scalability

The rapid pace of technological advancements introduces both opportunities and challenges for play-to-earn projects. Ensuring scalability and embracing emerging technologies are essential considerations to overcome potential limiting factors.

Integration with Layer 2 Solutions: Scalability has been a focal point for play-to-earn projects. Integration with Layer 2 solutions, such as sidechains and scaling protocols, aims to enhance transaction throughput and reduce fees, creating a more seamless and scalable gaming experience.

Embracing Blockchain Interoperability: Blockchain interoperability is emerging as a solution to potential scalability challenges. Play-to-earn projects are exploring cross-chain compatibility, allowing assets and data to flow seamlessly between different blockchain networks, expanding the scope and scalability of their ecosystems.

6. User Education and Onboarding Strategies

Questions about longevity often intersect with user education and onboarding strategies. Ensuring that participants have a clear understanding of play-to-earn models, blockchain technology, and associated risks is integral to fostering a knowledgeable and committed user base.

Comprehensive Educational Initiatives: Projects are investing in comprehensive educational initiatives to empower users with the knowledge needed to navigate the complexities of play-to-earn gaming. Resources, tutorials, and community-driven educational programs contribute to informed decision-making and sustained engagement.

Accessible Onboarding Processes: The onboarding process plays a crucial role in user retention. Simplifying and making the onboarding process accessible, especially for individuals new to blockchain and cryptocurrencies, enhances the inclusivity of play-to-earn ecosystems and supports long-term user growth.

7. Community Building and Governance Structures

The strength of the community and the effectiveness of governance structures contribute significantly to the longevity of play-to-earn projects. Actively fostering a sense of community and incorporating decentralized governance models are pivotal strategies for sustained success.

Community-Led Initiatives: Community-led initiatives go beyond economic considerations and contribute to the overall vibrancy of play-to-earn ecosystems. Projects that encourage community-driven events, collaborations, and initiatives create a dynamic and engaged user base that is more likely to persist over time.

Decentralized Governance Participation: Decentralized governance models empower users to participate in decision-making processes. Projects embracing this approach provide stakeholders with a sense of ownership and agency, fostering a collaborative environment that is less susceptible to centralized control and more resilient over the long term.

8. Lessons from Early Adoptions and Iterative Development

Drawing lessons from early adopters and engaging in iterative development are fundamental aspects of navigating questions about longevity. User feedback, market dynamics, and the evolving nature of play-to-earn gaming contribute to ongoing refinements and improvements.

Listening to User Feedback: User feedback is a valuable source of insights for play-to-earn projects. Actively listening to the experiences, concerns, and suggestions of early adopters enables projects to identify pain points, address challenges, and make informed decisions for sustained growth.

Iterative Development and Adaptability: The iterative development process is inherent to the evolution of play-to-earn gaming. Projects that embrace adaptability, iterate on their models, and incorporate lessons learned from challenges are better equipped to withstand the dynamic nature of the gaming and crypto markets.

Conclusion: Navigating the Journey Towards Longevity

The exploration of questions about longevity and limiting factors reveals the intricate landscape that play-to-earn projects must navigate. By proactively addressing economic sustainability, regulatory uncertainties, technological advancements, user education, and community building, projects lay the groundwork for a journey marked by resilience, adaptability, and enduring success. The subsequent chapters will further explore the ongoing evolution of play-to-earn gaming, examining broader impacts, innovations, and the maturation of play-to-earn economies.

Chapter 4 - Tokenomics and Blockchain Evolution Experimentation with New Token Models like Trove's Dual Token System

In the dynamic landscape of play-to-earn gaming, the exploration and experimentation with innovative token models play a pivotal role in shaping the economic foundations of these ecosystems. This section delves into the intricate details of Trove's dual token system, a pioneering example of how play-to-earn projects are pushing the boundaries of tokenomics to enhance sustainability, user engagement, and overall ecosystem health.

1. Trove's Dual Token System: A Paradigm Shift in Tokenomics

Trove's Vision and Objectives: Trove, as a leading play-to-earn project, set out to redefine traditional token models by introducing a dual token system. The vision behind this innovative approach aimed to address specific challenges prevalent in existing tokenomics and create a more balanced, sustainable, and user-centric gaming economy.

Key Objectives of the Dual Token System: The introduction of Trove's dual token system was driven by a set of key objectives. These objectives included mitigating economic imbalances, enhancing user incentives, fostering long-term engagement, and creating a model that adapts to the evolving needs of the play-to-earn community.

2. Understanding Trove's Dual Token System: Core Components

Trove's Native Token (TRO): At the core of Trove's dual token system is its native token, TRO. This primary token serves as the foundational currency within the ecosystem, facilitating transactions, enabling in-game purchases, and acting as a medium of exchange between players and the broader gaming economy.

Trove's Governance Token (TROV): Complementing TRO is Trove's governance token, TROV. Unlike TRO, TROV carries additional utility and governance functionalities. Holders of TROV are granted voting rights, allowing them to participate in critical decisions related to the project's development, economic models, and other governance-related matters.

3. Economic Sustainability through Dual Token Dynamics

Dynamic Tokenomics and Economic Resilience: The dual token system introduced by Trove adds a layer of dynamism to the project's tokenomics. This dynamism is designed to enhance economic resilience by adapting to market conditions, user behaviors, and the overall health of the play-to-earn ecosystem.

Balancing Supply and Demand: A key challenge in traditional token models is the balancing act between token supply and demand. Trove's dual token system addresses this challenge by allocating specific functions to each token, enabling a more nuanced approach to supply dynamics and economic equilibrium.

4. User Incentives and Participation: TRO as a Utility Token

TRO as a Utility Token: TRO, as Trove's primary utility token, serves as the lifeblood of in-game transactions and activities. Users engage with TRO for various in-game purchases, asset exchanges, and transactions within the Trove ecosystem. Its utility extends to diverse aspects of gameplay, from acquiring virtual assets to participating in decentralized finance (DeFi) protocols embedded in the Trove ecosystem.

Earning TRO through Gameplay: One of the innovative aspects of Trove's dual token system is the emphasis on earning TRO through active gameplay. Users are incentivized to participate in various in-game activities, contributing to the overall vibrancy of the ecosystem while earning rewards in the form of TRO.

5. Governance Empowerment: TROV as a Governance Token

TROV's Role in Governance: TROV, as Trove's governance token, introduces a novel dimension to user engagement. Beyond its economic utility, TROV empowers users with the ability to participate in governance decisions. Holders of TROV have voting rights, allowing them to influence the direction of the project, propose changes, and actively contribute to the decision-making processes.

Decentralized Decision-Making: The incorporation of TROV in Trove's dual token system signifies a commitment to decentralized decision-making. By distributing governance authority among token holders, Trove aims to create a more democratic and community-driven model, aligning the project's trajectory with the collective interests of its users.

6. Trove's Approach to Sustainability and Anti-Inflation Measures

Sustainability Through Economic Diversity: The dual token system contributes to Trove's sustainability by fostering economic diversity within the ecosystem. TRO and TROV, with their distinct roles, work in tandem to create a more resilient and adaptable economic model, reducing the reliance on a single token for all functions.

Anti-Inflation Measures and Economic Stability: Inflationary pressures are a common concern in token economies. Trove's dual token system incorporates anti-inflation measures to manage token supply effectively. By aligning token issuance with user participation and economic activities, Trove aims to maintain economic stability and prevent excessive inflation.

7. Lessons Learned: Iterative Development and Community Feedback

Iterative Development Based on User Insights: Trove's journey with the dual token system exemplifies the importance of iterative development. By actively listening to user feedback, observing market dynamics, and learning from the experiences of the community, Trove has iteratively refined its dual token model to address emerging challenges and enhance user satisfaction.

Community-Driven Enhancements: Community feedback plays a central role in the evolution of Trove's dual token system. Engaging with the user community allows Trove to identify areas for improvement, understand user preferences, and implement changes that align with the collective vision of the play-to-earn ecosystem.

8. The Broader Impact on Play-to-Earn Tokenomics

Trove's Influence on Industry Trends: As a trailblazer in the play-to-earn space, Trove's dual token system has the potential to influence broader industry trends. The success and innovations introduced by Trove may inspire other play-to-earn projects to explore diverse tokenomics models, fostering a landscape of continuous experimentation and improvement.

Encouraging Diversity in Token Models: The introduction of Trove's dual token system encourages diversity in token models within the play-to-earn sector. This diversity is essential for the maturation of the industry, allowing projects to tailor their tokenomics to specific needs, challenges, and aspirations, contributing to a more resilient and innovative ecosystem.

Conclusion: Trove's Dual Token System and the Future of Play-to-Earn Tokenomics

Trove's dual token system stands as a beacon of innovation in the realm of play-to-earn tokenomics. By addressing economic challenges, enhancing user incentives, and empowering the community through decentralized governance, Trove exemplifies how thoughtful experimentation can pave the way for a more sustainable, engaging, and enduring future for play-to-earn gaming. The subsequent chapters will further explore the evolving landscape of tokenomics and the broader impacts on play-to-earn economies.

Attempts to Improve Sustainability and Manage Inflation

In the dynamic and evolving landscape of play-to-earn gaming, the sustainability of tokenomics models is a critical consideration. This section explores various attempts made by play-to-earn projects to enhance sustainability and manage inflation within their ecosystems. From innovative tokenomic structures to anti-inflation measures, these efforts play a crucial role in shaping the long-term viability of play-to-earn gaming.

1. The Challenge of Inflation in Token Economies

Understanding Inflation in Play-to-Earn Models: Inflation, the increase in the supply of a token, poses challenges to the stability and sustainability of play-to-earn ecosystems. Unchecked inflation can lead to a devaluation of in-game assets, impacting the economic incentives for players and potentially eroding the overall value of the token.

Balancing Token Issuance and User Participation: Projects face the delicate task of balancing token issuance with user participation. Overly aggressive token issuance can lead to inflation, while insufficient issuance may hinder user incentives. Striking the right balance is crucial for maintaining a healthy and sustainable token economy.

2. Innovations in Tokenomic Structures

Introduction to Innovative Tokenomic Structures: To address the challenge of inflation and improve sustainability, play-to-earn projects have been experimenting with innovative tokenomic structures. These structures aim to create a more dynamic and adaptable economic model that aligns with the evolving needs of the gaming community.

Dynamic Supply Mechanisms: Some projects have introduced dynamic supply mechanisms, where token issuance adjusts based on factors such as user activity, ecosystem health, and market conditions. This dynamic approach aims to prevent excessive inflation while promoting economic resilience.

3. Staking and Lock-Up Mechanisms

Role of Staking in Anti-Inflation Strategies: Staking mechanisms allow users to lock up their tokens for a specified period, contributing to anti-inflation strategies. By incentivizing users to stake their tokens, projects can reduce circulating supply, create scarcity, and mitigate inflationary pressures.

Lock-Up Periods and Reward Structures: Projects implement varying lock-up periods and reward structures to encourage token staking. Longer lock-up periods often come with higher rewards, providing users with an economic incentive to commit to the ecosystem for an extended duration, promoting stability and sustainability.

4. Burn Mechanisms and Deflationary Strategies

Token Burning as a Deflationary Measure: Token burning involves removing a portion of the token supply from circulation, creating a deflationary effect. Some play-to-earn projects incorporate burn mechanisms as a strategy to counter inflation and enhance the scarcity of their native tokens.

Strategic Burn Events and Community Involvement: Projects may organize strategic burn events, where tokens are intentionally destroyed, aligning with specific milestones or achievements. Involving the community in decision-making around burn events fosters a sense of ownership and collective responsibility for the economic health of the ecosystem.

5. Integration with Decentralized Finance (DeFi) Protocols

Utilizing DeFi Protocols for Sustainability: The integration of decentralized finance (DeFi) protocols provides play-to-earn projects with additional tools for managing inflation and enhancing sustainability. Yield farming, liquidity provision, and other DeFi strategies can contribute to a more robust economic model.

Leveraging DeFi for Liquidity and Stability: By leveraging DeFi, projects can enhance liquidity, stabilize token prices, and create additional revenue streams. The synergy between play-to-earn gaming and DeFi introduces innovative financial instruments that contribute to the overall economic resilience of the ecosystem.

6. Governance-Driven Economic Adjustments

Decentralized Governance for Economic Adaptations: Projects embracing decentralized governance models empower the community to participate in decisions related to economic adjustments. Governance-driven approaches allow for collective decision-making on parameters such as token issuance, inflation targets, and other economic policies.

Balancing Community Input and Expertise: Effectively balancing community input with expert insights is crucial in governance-driven economic adjustments. Projects must create mechanisms for informed decision-making, ensuring that economic policies align with the project's long-term vision and the diverse interests of the community.

7. Tokenomics Transparency and Communication

Importance of Transparent Tokenomics: Transparent communication about tokenomics is essential for building trust and confidence within the play-to-earn community. Projects that openly share information about token issuance schedules, inflation targets, and economic adjustments contribute to a more informed and engaged user base.

Educational Initiatives on Tokenomics: To enhance transparency, projects often invest in educational initiatives focused on tokenomics. Tutorials, guides, and community-driven educational programs help users understand the economic principles that govern play-to-earn ecosystems, fostering a more knowledgeable and empowered community.

8. Navigating Challenges: Lessons Learned

Iterative Development and Learning from Challenges: The journey to improve sustainability and manage inflation in play-to-earn tokenomics involves iterative development and continuous learning. Projects that actively seek feedback, observe market dynamics, and learn from challenges are better equipped to refine their economic models and ensure long-term viability.

Community Collaboration and Adaptability: Collaboration with the community and an adaptable mindset are fundamental in navigating challenges. Play-to-earn projects that foster a collaborative environment, listen to community insights, and adapt their tokenomics based on collective experiences are more likely to thrive in the ever-evolving landscape.

9. The Broader Impact on Play-to-Earn Economics

Influence on Industry Trends: Projects pioneering innovative anti-inflation measures and sustainable tokenomics have the potential to influence industry trends. Their successes and lessons learned contribute to the maturation of play-to-earn economics, inspiring other projects to explore diverse strategies for economic resilience.

Encouraging Diverse Approaches: The attempts to improve sustainability and manage inflation contribute to the diversification of approaches within the play-to-earn sector. Encouraging diverse economic models fosters a resilient ecosystem where projects can tailor their tokenomics to specific needs, challenges, and aspirations.

Conclusion: Shaping the Future of Play-to-Earn Tokenomics

Efforts to improve sustainability and manage inflation in play-to-earn tokenomics represent a dynamic and ongoing journey. From innovative tokenomic structures to community-driven governance and transparency initiatives, these endeavors shape the future of play-to-earn gaming, creating a more resilient, adaptable, and sustainable economic landscape. The subsequent chapters will explore further dimensions of play-to-earn economics, including the impact on gameplay, user experiences, and the broader implications for the gaming industry.

Integration with Layer 2 Networks like ImmutableX for Scalability

The pursuit of scalability is a paramount concern in the realm of play-to-earn gaming, and one innovative solution gaining prominence is the integration of Layer 2 networks. This section explores the intricacies of this integration, focusing on platforms such as ImmutableX and their role in enhancing scalability within play-to-earn ecosystems.

1. Understanding the Scalability Challenge in Play-to-Earn Gaming

Scalability as a Crucial Factor: The surge in popularity of play-to-earn gaming has underscored the need for scalable blockchain solutions. Traditional blockchains, while providing security and decentralization, often face challenges in handling the transaction throughput required for a seamless and responsive gaming experience.

Impact of Scalability on User Experience: Scalability directly influences the user experience in play-to-earn games. Long transaction times, high fees, and network congestion can hinder the fluidity of gameplay, discouraging user engagement and limiting the growth potential of play-to-earn ecosystems.

2. Layer 2 Networks: A Solution for Scalability Challenges

Introduction to Layer 2 Scaling: Layer 2 scaling solutions are designed to address the scalability limitations of main blockchain networks. These solutions operate "on top" of the main blockchain, offering a more efficient and faster environment for processing transactions without compromising the security and decentralization provided by the underlying blockchain.

Key Characteristics of Layer 2 Networks: Layer 2 networks boast key characteristics such as faster transaction speeds, lower fees, and increased scalability. By offloading a significant portion of transactional activity from the main blockchain, Layer 2 solutions aim to create a more responsive and cost-effective infrastructure for play-to-earn gaming.

3. ImmutableX: Revolutionizing Play-to-Earn Scalability

Overview of ImmutableX: ImmutableX stands out as a leading Layer 2 scaling solution, specifically tailored for the needs of play-to-earn gaming. Its architecture, based on zk-rollups, offers a unique blend of scalability, security, and decentralization, making it an attractive option for play-to-earn projects seeking to enhance their infrastructure.

Zero Gas Fees and Instant Transactions: ImmutableX's implementation of zk-rollups brings forth the promise of zero gas fees and near-instant transaction confirmation. This transformative feature directly addresses the challenges of high fees and slow transaction speeds that have plagued traditional blockchain networks, providing a frictionless experience for players.

4. Benefits and Advantages of ImmutableX Integration

Seamless User Experience: The integration of ImmutableX contributes to a seamless user experience, a critical factor for the success of play-to-earn games. With zero gas fees and rapid transaction confirmations, players can engage in in-game transactions and activities without the delays and costs associated with traditional blockchain networks.

Enhanced Scalability for Gaming Activities: ImmutableX's scalability enhancements extend to gaming activities, allowing for a higher volume of transactions and interactions within the play-to-earn ecosystem. This scalability is particularly crucial for games with intricate economies, decentralized asset exchanges, and a high frequency of in-game transactions.

5. NFT Minting and Trading on ImmutableX

Efficient NFT Minting: ImmutableX's Layer 2 architecture streamlines the process of NFT minting. The efficiency of zk-rollups enables rapid and cost-effective creation of non-fungible tokens (NFTs), empowering game developers to seamlessly integrate unique and scarce digital assets into their play-to-earn environments.

Instantaneous NFT Trading: ImmutableX's Layer 2 infrastructure facilitates near-instantaneous NFT trading. This not only enhances the user experience by eliminating the delays associated with traditional blockchain networks but also opens up new possibilities for dynamic in-game markets, fostering a vibrant virtual economy.

6. Decentralization and Security Considerations

Preserving Decentralization: ImmutableX places a strong emphasis on preserving decentralization despite its Layer 2 nature. The underlying zk-rollup technology ensures that the security and decentralization principles of the Ethereum blockchain are maintained, providing a robust foundation for play-to-earn projects.

Smart Contract Functionality: ImmutableX supports smart contract functionality within its Layer 2 framework. This capability is essential for play-to-earn games that rely on smart contracts to execute complex in-game logic, enabling developers to maintain the programmability and flexibility of Ethereum while benefiting from Layer 2 scalability.

7. Developer Adoption and Ecosystem Growth

Attracting Play-to-Earn Projects: The appeal of zero gas fees, instant transactions, and scalability positions ImmutableX as an attractive solution for play-to-earn projects. The platform has seen significant adoption from game developers seeking to enhance the scalability of their ecosystems and improve the overall gaming experience for players.

Creating a Thriving Ecosystem: ImmutableX's integration contributes to the creation of a thriving ecosystem of play-to-earn games. As more projects adopt this Layer 2 solution, interoperability and shared standards can emerge, fostering a network effect that benefits both developers and players within the play-to-earn space.

8. Challenges and Considerations in Layer 2 Integration

Integration Complexity and Development Efforts: While Layer 2 solutions offer substantial benefits, the integration process can present complexities for developers. Adapting existing games or developing new ones to leverage Layer 2 scalability requires careful planning, development efforts, and considerations of interoperability with other blockchain components.

User Education and Onboarding: The shift to Layer 2 networks necessitates user education and onboarding initiatives. Ensuring that players understand the benefits of the new infrastructure, how to interact with Layer 2-compatible wallets, and the overall impact on their gaming experience is vital for a smooth transition.

9. ImmutableX's Role in Shaping the Future of Play-to-Earn Gaming

Influence on Industry Trends: ImmutableX's role in play-to-earn gaming extends beyond its technical contributions. The platform's success and adoption set a precedent for the industry, influencing trends and encouraging other Layer 2 solutions to emerge, each vying to enhance scalability and redefine the gaming experience.

Continuous Innovation and Iterative Development: ImmutableX's journey is marked by continuous innovation and iterative development. As the platform evolves, it is likely to introduce new features, optimizations, and collaborations, contributing to the ongoing maturation of Layer 2 solutions and their integration into the broader play-to-earn gaming landscape.

Conclusion: ImmutableX and the Scalable Future of Play-to-Earn Gaming

The integration of Layer 2 networks, exemplified by platforms like ImmutableX, marks a pivotal advancement in addressing the scalability challenges inherent in play-to-earn gaming. As the industry continues to explore and adopt scalable solutions, the collaboration between Layer 2 networks and play-to-earn projects promises a future where users experience seamless, cost-effective, and scalable gameplay. Subsequent chapters will delve into additional dimensions of play-to-earn blockchain evolution, including the impact on tokenomics, gameplay, and the broader gaming industry.

Leveraging Decentralized Finance (DeFi) Protocols and DAO Structures

The intersection of play-to-earn gaming and decentralized finance (DeFi) introduces a new frontier in blockchain evolution. This section explores how play-to-earn projects are leveraging DeFi protocols and decentralized autonomous organization (DAO) structures to enhance tokenomics, governance, and user engagement within their ecosystems.

1. The Convergence of Play-to-Earn and DeFi

Understanding DeFi in the Context of Play-to-Earn: Decentralized finance (DeFi) represents a set of financial tools and services built on blockchain technology, aiming to recreate traditional financial systems in a trustless and permissionless manner. When integrated into play-to-earn gaming, DeFi introduces novel opportunities for enhancing economic models and user experiences.

Strategic Integration: Play-to-earn projects strategically integrate DeFi protocols to tap into the liquidity, composability, and programmability offered by these financial instruments. The synergy between play-to-earn and DeFi introduces innovative economic structures, fostering a more dynamic and user-centric gaming ecosystem.

2. Tokenomics Enhanced by DeFi Mechanisms

Introduction to DeFi Mechanisms in Tokenomics: DeFi mechanisms, such as liquidity pools, yield farming, and decentralized exchanges, provide play-to-earn projects with tools to enhance tokenomics. These mechanisms introduce additional revenue streams, economic incentives, and opportunities for users to participate in the financial aspects of the gaming ecosystem.

Liquidity Pools and Token Swapping: Liquidity pools, a common DeFi feature, enable users to provide liquidity to decentralized exchanges. Play-to-earn projects leverage these pools to facilitate token swapping within the gaming ecosystem, allowing users to seamlessly trade in-game assets or tokens with reduced slippage.

3. Yield Farming and Staking Strategies

Yield Farming as an Economic Driver: Yield farming involves users staking their tokens in decentralized protocols in exchange for additional token rewards. Play-to-earn projects integrate yield farming to incentivize user participation, creating a virtuous cycle where players are rewarded for contributing to the liquidity and vibrancy of the in-game economy.

Staking Strategies for Long-Term Engagement: Staking strategies, another DeFi mechanism, encourage long-term user engagement. By allowing players to stake their tokens for a specific period, projects incentivize commitment to the ecosystem, enhancing economic stability and fostering a sense of ownership among participants.

4. Decentralized Exchanges (DEX) in Play-to-Earn Gaming

Introduction to Decentralized Exchanges: Decentralized exchanges (DEX) enable peer-to-peer trading of tokens without the need for intermediaries. Play-to-earn projects integrate DEX to provide users with a seamless and decentralized platform for trading in-game assets, enhancing user autonomy and reducing reliance on traditional centralized exchanges.

User Benefits and Security: DEX integration benefits users by providing a secure and trustless environment for trading. Players can retain control of their assets and participate in the decentralized economy of play-to-earn games without the concerns associated with centralized exchanges.

5. Governance and Decision-Making through DAO Structures

Decentralized Autonomous Organizations (DAOs) in Gaming: DAO structures empower the community to participate in governance and decision-making processes. Play-to-earn projects implement DAO structures to distribute decision-making authority, giving users a voice in matters such as protocol upgrades, economic policies, and in-game governance.

DAO Governance Tokens: Projects often introduce governance tokens within DAO structures. These tokens grant holders the right to vote on proposals, shaping the future direction of the ecosystem. DAO governance tokens become a valuable asset, aligning the interests of the community with the success and sustainability of the play-to-earn project.

6. Collaborative Development and Community Involvement

Community-Led Development Initiatives: DAO structures encourage community-led development initiatives. Play-to-earn projects that embrace decentralized governance empower users to propose and vote on improvements, features, and changes to the ecosystem. This collaborative approach fosters a sense of ownership and inclusivity among the community.

Incentivizing Participation through DAOs: To incentivize participation in DAOs, projects often allocate rewards or governance tokens to users actively engaged in decision-making processes. This incentivization model promotes a vibrant and participatory community, contributing to the overall health and sustainability of the play-to-earn ecosystem.

7. Challenges and Considerations in DeFi and DAO Integration

Complexity of DeFi Integration: While the benefits of integrating DeFi and DAO structures are evident, the complexity of implementation poses challenges for play-to-earn projects. The need for secure smart contract development, user education, and seamless integration with existing gaming systems requires careful planning and execution.

Ensuring User Understanding of DeFi and DAOs: User education is crucial to ensure that players understand the functionalities and benefits of DeFi mechanisms and DAO structures. Projects must provide clear documentation, tutorials, and support to help users navigate the decentralized financial landscape and actively participate in governance.

8. Real-World Impact on User Engagement and Retention

Sustainable User Engagement: The integration of DeFi and DAO structures contributes to sustainable user engagement. By providing additional avenues for users to participate in the economic aspects of play-to-earn gaming, projects create a more immersive and rewarding experience, fostering long-term player commitment.

Building a Loyal Community: Projects that successfully leverage DeFi and DAOs often build a loyal and dedicated community. The sense of community ownership, coupled with the economic benefits offered through DeFi mechanisms, creates an environment where users feel invested in the success and growth of the play-to-earn ecosystem.

9. Influence on Tokenomics and Economic Models

Evolving Tokenomics through DeFi Integration: The integration of DeFi mechanisms reshapes tokenomics, introducing new dynamics and revenue streams. Projects that effectively leverage these mechanisms create economic models that adapt to user behaviors, market conditions, and the evolving landscape of play-to-earn gaming.

Impact on Economic Sustainability: DeFi integration contributes to economic sustainability by diversifying revenue sources and providing mechanisms for users to actively contribute to the ecosystem. The continuous evolution of economic models through DeFi mechanisms ensures adaptability and resilience in the face of changing market dynamics.

Conclusion: The Synergy of DeFi and DAOs in Play-to-Earn Gaming

The synergy between play-to-earn gaming, decentralized finance (DeFi) protocols, and decentralized autonomous organization (DAO) structures marks a transformative evolution in blockchain technology. As play-to-earn projects continue to explore and implement these innovative mechanisms, the resulting economic models, user experiences, and community dynamics shape a future where players are not just participants but active contributors to the success and governance of play-to-earn ecosystems. Subsequent chapters will delve into further dimensions of blockchain evolution within the play-to-earn gaming landscape, including the impact on gameplay, adoption, and the broader gaming industry.

Contributions and Limitations of Blockchain Technology

Blockchain technology underpins the transformative evolution of play-to-earn gaming, introducing a paradigm shift in how digital economies are structured and operated. This section explores the multifaceted contributions and limitations of blockchain technology within the context of play-to-earn gaming ecosystems.

1. Contributions of Blockchain Technology in Play-to-Earn Gaming

Decentralization and Trustless Transactions: One of the primary contributions of blockchain technology to play-to-earn gaming is the establishment of decentralization. By utilizing distributed ledger technology, blockchain ensures that in-game assets and transactions are trustlessly recorded, eliminating the need for central authorities and enhancing security and transparency.

Ownership and True Scarcity of Digital Assets: Blockchain introduces the concept of true ownership of digital assets through non-fungible tokens (NFTs). Players in play-to-earn games can genuinely own and trade NFTs representing in-game items, characters, and assets, fostering a sense of value and scarcity in the digital realm.

Immutable Smart Contracts and Transparency: Smart contracts on the blockchain are immutable and transparent, ensuring that the rules governing play-to-earn games are tamper-proof. This contributes to fair play, as the predefined rules are executed without bias or interference, instilling trust among players in the integrity of the gaming environment.

2. Enabling Play-to-Earn Models through Tokenization

Tokenization of In-Game Assets: Blockchain facilitates the tokenization of in-game assets, enabling the representation of virtual items as tradable tokens on the blockchain. This tokenization forms the basis of play-to-earn models, allowing players to earn and trade digital assets with real-world value.

Dynamic Economies and Player Incentives: The tokenization of in-game assets leads to the creation of dynamic virtual economies. Players are incentivized to actively participate in the game, contributing to the growth of the ecosystem and earning tokens as rewards. This economic model aligns the interests of players with the success of the play-to-earn project.

3. Interoperability and Cross-Game Asset Exchange

Interoperability Across Games: Blockchain technology introduces interoperability, allowing players to use their in-game assets across different games and platforms. This cross-game asset exchange enhances the versatility and value of virtual items, offering players more opportunities to leverage their digital holdings.

Creating a Unified Metaverse: The interoperability facilitated by blockchain contributes to the vision of a unified metaverse. Players can seamlessly navigate between different virtual worlds, bringing their assets and achievements with them. This interconnected metaverse enhances the overall gaming experience and opens up new possibilities for player interaction.

4. Decentralized Finance (DeFi) Integration for Economic Depth

DeFi Protocols Enhancing Economic Models: Blockchain's integration with decentralized finance (DeFi) protocols introduces economic depth to play-to-earn ecosystems. DeFi mechanisms such as liquidity pools, yield farming, and decentralized exchanges offer additional avenues for users to engage with the economic aspects of play-to-earn gaming, contributing to a more vibrant and dynamic ecosystem.

Unlocking New Revenue Streams: DeFi integration unlocks new revenue streams within play-to-earn gaming. Players can participate in yield farming, stake their in-game tokens, and contribute to liquidity pools, earning additional rewards beyond traditional gameplay. This diversification of income sources enhances the sustainability of play-to-earn models.

5. Decentralized Governance Models and Community Empowerment

Decentralized Autonomous Organizations (DAOs): Blockchain introduces decentralized autonomous organizations (DAOs) to play-to-earn projects, enabling community-driven governance. DAOs empower players to participate in decision-making processes, vote on protocol upgrades, and collectively shape the future of the gaming ecosystem.

Community Empowerment and Inclusivity: Decentralized governance fosters community empowerment and inclusivity. Players become active contributors to the development and governance of the play-to-earn project, creating a sense of ownership and fostering a collaborative environment where diverse voices are heard.

6. Limitations and Challenges of Blockchain Technology

Scalability Concerns: One of the significant limitations of blockchain technology is scalability. The current limitations in transaction throughput and latency can pose challenges for play-to-earn gaming, especially during periods of high user activity. Addressing scalability concerns is crucial for ensuring a seamless and responsive gaming experience.

Environmental Impact: The energy consumption associated with some blockchain consensus mechanisms, such as Proof of Work (PoW), raises environmental concerns. Play-to-earn projects built on energy-intensive blockchains may face scrutiny due to their carbon footprint. The industry is actively exploring eco-friendly alternatives, such as Proof of Stake (PoS), to mitigate this challenge.

7. Security and Smart Contract Risks

Smart Contract Vulnerabilities: While smart contracts offer immutability and transparency, they are not immune to vulnerabilities. The presence of bugs or vulnerabilities in smart contracts can lead to security breaches, exploitation, and financial losses. Ensuring the robustness of smart contract code is paramount for the security of play-to-earn projects.

Phishing and User Education: The decentralized nature of blockchain introduces risks such as phishing attacks. Players may be targeted by malicious actors attempting to exploit vulnerabilities or deceive them into revealing sensitive information. User education and robust security measures are essential to mitigate these risks.

8. Regulatory Uncertainty and Compliance Challenges

Global Regulatory Landscape: Blockchain technology operates in a global context with varying regulatory frameworks. Play-to-earn projects may encounter challenges related to regulatory uncertainty, compliance requirements, and legal considerations. Navigating this complex landscape requires proactive engagement with regulatory authorities and adherence to evolving compliance standards.

Potential for Regulatory Scrutiny: The innovative nature of play-to-earn gaming built on blockchain technology may attract regulatory scrutiny. Projects must stay abreast of legal developments, work towards compliance, and engage in transparent communication to address potential concerns from regulatory authorities.

9. User Experience and Onboarding Hurdles

Custodial Wallets and Complexity: The use of blockchain technology often involves interacting with digital wallets. While custodial wallets simplify the onboarding process, they introduce custodial risks. Non-custodial wallets, on the other hand, offer more security but may be perceived as complex for new users. Balancing security and user experience remains a challenge.

Educational Barriers: Blockchain technology introduces new concepts and terminologies that may be unfamiliar to mainstream users. Overcoming educational barriers and providing user-friendly resources are essential for facilitating widespread adoption of play-to-earn gaming and blockchain technology.

10. Future Innovations and Mitigations

Technological Advancements and Solutions: The limitations and challenges of blockchain technology are not static. Ongoing technological advancements, research, and development efforts are focused on addressing scalability concerns, improving environmental sustainability, enhancing security measures, and simplifying user interfaces. Future innovations hold the potential to mitigate existing challenges.

Collaboration and Industry Best Practices: The blockchain and play-to-earn gaming industries are collaborative spaces where projects, developers, and stakeholders share insights and best practices. Collaborative efforts, industry standards, and the adoption of best practices contribute to the continuous improvement and maturation of blockchain technology within the gaming landscape.

Conclusion: Navigating the Evolving Landscape

Blockchain technology stands as a cornerstone in the evolution of play-to-earn gaming, offering unprecedented opportunities and introducing new complexities. Understanding the contributions and limitations of blockchain is essential for navigating the evolving landscape of play-to-earn ecosystems. As the industry continues to innovate and address challenges, blockchain technology remains a dynamic force shaping the future of digital economies within the gaming sphere.

Chapter 5 - Improving Gameplay and Design
Developing More Compelling Gameplay Mechanics and Genres

Enhancing gameplay mechanics and diversifying gaming genres are pivotal aspects in the evolution of play-to-earn gaming. This chapter explores the strategies, innovations, and considerations involved in developing more compelling gameplay experiences, attracting a broader audience, and ensuring the long-term engagement of players within the play-to-earn ecosystem.

1. Evolution of Gameplay in Play-to-Earn Models

Understanding Play-to-Earn Gameplay: Play-to-earn gaming fundamentally transforms traditional gaming by introducing economic incentives for players. Beyond the conventional enjoyment of gameplay, users can earn tangible rewards, creating a dynamic and participatory gaming experience.

Incentivizing Player Actions: Successful play-to-earn models incentivize a variety of player actions, from completing in-game challenges to contributing to the ecosystem's growth. This evolution necessitates a rethinking of traditional gameplay mechanics to align with the economic principles that underpin play-to-earn gaming.

2. Dynamic Gameplay Mechanics for Enhanced Engagement

Quests, Challenges, and Achievements: Implementing quests, challenges, and achievements within play-to-earn games enhances player engagement. By offering rewards for completing specific tasks, developers encourage users to explore the game world, interact with in-game assets, and contribute to the overall vibrancy of the ecosystem.

Skill-Based and Competitive Gameplay: Introducing skill-based and competitive elements elevates the gameplay experience. Play-to-earn games can incorporate skill challenges, tournaments, and leaderboards, providing players with opportunities to showcase their abilities and earn rewards based on performance.

3. Gamification of Economic Activities

Integrating Economic Activities: To align with the economic principles of play-to-earn, developers gamify economic activities within the game. This includes mechanisms such as virtual trading, resource management, and economic strategy, creating a seamless integration of in-game economics with player progression.

Strategic Decision-Making: Play-to-earn games evolve beyond simple resource gathering to involve strategic decision-making. Players may need to make informed choices about asset management, investments, and in-game actions, introducing a layer of complexity that adds depth to the overall gaming experience.

4. Fusion of Play-to-Earn with Traditional Genres

Action, Adventure, and RPG Integration: The fusion of play-to-earn mechanics with traditional gaming genres such as action, adventure, and role-playing games (RPGs) broadens the appeal of play-to-earn gaming. Players experience familiar and immersive gameplay while also benefiting from economic incentives.

Simulation and Strategy Elements: Simulation and strategy elements contribute to the play-to-earn landscape by providing players with opportunities to simulate real-world scenarios or engage in strategic decision-making. This integration enhances both the entertainment value and the economic dimensions of gameplay.

5. Non-Fungible Tokens (NFTs) and Gameplay Integration

Dynamic NFT-Based Assets: Non-fungible tokens (NFTs) represent unique and scarce digital assets, and their integration into gameplay introduces dynamic and valuable in-game items. From character skins to rare weapons, NFT-based assets contribute to the diversity of gameplay experiences.

In-Game NFT Utility: NFTs within play-to-earn games can offer utility beyond simple ownership. Developers can design gameplay mechanics that leverage NFT attributes, such as special abilities tied to specific NFTs or the combination of multiple NFTs unlocking unique features.

6. User-Centric Design for Inclusivity

Appealing to Casual Gamers: To broaden the player base, play-to-earn games need to appeal to casual gamers. User-centric design, intuitive interfaces, and accessible gameplay mechanics are essential elements in ensuring that even those unfamiliar with blockchain technology can easily navigate and enjoy the gaming experience.

Balancing Complexity and Accessibility: Achieving a balance between the complexity required for play-to-earn economics and the accessibility demanded by a diverse player base is crucial. Developers must design gameplay systems that offer depth for experienced users while remaining intuitive for newcomers.

7. Cross-Platform Integration for Seamless Experiences

Mobile, PC, and Console Integration: To maximize accessibility and player engagement, play-to-earn games should integrate seamlessly across various platforms, including mobile devices, PCs, and consoles. Cross-platform compatibility ensures that players can participate in the play-to-earn ecosystem regardless of their preferred gaming device.

Progression Synchronization: Synchronizing player progression and in-game assets across different platforms enhances the overall gaming experience. Players should be able to seamlessly transition between devices while retaining their earned rewards and achievements, fostering a continuous and integrated gaming journey.

8. Innovations in Augmented Reality (AR) and Virtual Reality (VR)

AR and VR Integration: The integration of augmented reality (AR) and virtual reality (VR) technologies introduces innovative dimensions to play-to-earn gaming. AR enhances real-world interactions with in-game assets, while VR immerses players in virtual environments, providing novel and immersive play-to-earn experiences.

Immersive In-Game Economies: AR and VR technologies enable the creation of immersive in-game economies. Players can experience a more tactile and visually rich representation of their virtual assets, fostering a deeper connection to the play-to-earn ecosystem and its economic dynamics.

9. Community-Driven Content Creation and Modding

Player-Created Content: Empowering players to create and contribute content enhances the richness of play-to-earn ecosystems. Games can incorporate features that allow users to create their own quests, challenges, or even design in-game items, fostering a collaborative environment where players actively shape the gaming experience.

Modding Support and Customization: Providing modding support enables players to customize their gaming experience. From creating unique in-game assets to modifying gameplay mechanics, modding support adds a layer of personalization, encouraging player creativity and contributing to the longevity of play-to-earn games.

10. Balancing Playability and Earnings Potential

Ensuring a Fun and Rewarding Experience: While economic incentives are a central aspect of play-to-earn gaming, ensuring a fun and rewarding experience is paramount. Developers must strike a balance between playability, entertainment value, and the potential for earnings to create a holistic and engaging gaming environment.

Iterative Design and Player Feedback: An iterative design approach, informed by player feedback, is crucial for refining gameplay mechanics. Developers should actively seek input from the community, analyze player behavior, and make adjustments to ensure that the gameplay aligns with user expectations and preferences.

As play-to-earn gaming continues to evolve, the development of compelling gameplay mechanics and the exploration of diverse gaming genres play pivotal roles in shaping the industry's future. By prioritizing user engagement, inclusivity, and innovation, developers contribute to the creation of immersive and rewarding play-to-earn experiences that captivate a global audience.

Focus on Casual Gamers vs. Just Crypto Natives

Balancing the appeal of play-to-earn gaming between casual gamers and crypto natives is a critical consideration for the sustainable growth and widespread adoption of these innovative ecosystems. This chapter explores the strategies, challenges, and implications of designing play-to-earn games that cater to both casual gamers, who may be new to blockchain technology, and crypto natives who are familiar with the intricacies of decentralized ecosystems.

1. Understanding the Casual Gamer Landscape

Defining Casual Gamers: Casual gamers are individuals who play games infrequently and often for short periods. They may not have extensive gaming experience or be familiar with blockchain technology. Understanding the preferences and habits of this demographic is crucial for creating play-to-earn games that resonate with a broader audience.

Appealing Game Mechanics for Casual Gamers: Casual gamers typically gravitate towards straightforward and easily understandable game mechanics. Games with intuitive controls, simple objectives, and a low learning curve are more likely to capture and retain the interest of casual players.

2. Onboarding Strategies for Casual Gamers

Simplified Onboarding Processes: To attract casual gamers, play-to-earn games should implement simplified onboarding processes. Clear and user-friendly interfaces, step-by-step tutorials, and guided experiences can help ease casual players into the world of blockchain gaming without overwhelming them with technical details.

Intuitive Wallet Integration: Casual gamers may not be familiar with cryptocurrency wallets. Integrating intuitive and user-friendly wallet solutions within the game interface streamlines the onboarding process, reducing friction for new users who may be exploring blockchain technology for the first time.

3. Designing In-Game Economics for Accessibility

Low-Entry Barriers: Play-to-earn games targeting casual gamers should have low-entry barriers. This includes affordable in-game assets, minimal transaction costs, and straightforward economic models that are easy for newcomers to grasp. Keeping the initial investment manageable encourages casual players to participate.

Accessible Tokenomics: Designing accessible tokenomics involves creating a clear connection between in-game activities and tangible rewards. Casual gamers should easily understand how their actions within the game translate into earnings, fostering a sense of accomplishment and incentivizing continued engagement.

4. Gamifying Economic Participation for Casual Players

Incentivizing Basic Actions: To keep casual gamers engaged, play-to-earn games can incentivize basic in-game actions. Simple tasks, such as completing quests, exploring the game world, or interacting with other players, can earn rewards. This gamification encourages regular participation without requiring an in-depth understanding of blockchain concepts.

Engagement Rewards Over Complex Strategies: Rather than focusing on complex economic strategies, play-to-earn games for casual gamers can emphasize engagement rewards. Regular play and social interactions within the game can be the primary drivers of earnings, making the experience more about enjoyment and less about intricate financial maneuvers.

5. Educating Casual Gamers on Blockchain Basics

Integrating Educational Elements: Casual gamers may be unfamiliar with blockchain technology. Integrating educational elements within the game, such as pop-up tips, interactive guides, or optional tutorials, can gradually introduce basic blockchain concepts without overwhelming the player.

Community Learning Spaces: Establishing community learning spaces within the game environment allows casual gamers to interact with more experienced players or community moderators who can provide guidance and answer questions. This informal learning approach fosters a supportive environment for newcomers.

6. Catering to the Crypto Native Audience

Defining Crypto Natives: Crypto natives are individuals with a deep understanding of blockchain technology and cryptocurrency. They are likely familiar with the complexities of decentralized systems, tokenomics, and the principles of play-to-earn models. Designing for crypto natives involves catering to their specific expectations and preferences.

Advanced Gameplay Mechanics: For crypto natives, play-to-earn games can incorporate more advanced gameplay mechanics. This includes intricate economic strategies, decentralized finance (DeFi) interactions within the game, and the utilization of blockchain features such as smart contracts for complex in-game agreements.

7. Providing Deeper Economic Opportunities for Crypto Natives

Complex Tokenomics and Investment Strategies: Play-to-earn games targeting crypto natives can offer more complex tokenomics and investment strategies. This includes opportunities for yield farming, liquidity provision, and advanced trading mechanisms within the in-game economy. Providing deeper economic opportunities aligns with the preferences of users experienced in decentralized finance.

Interoperability with External Platforms: Catering to crypto natives involves considering interoperability with external platforms. Players familiar with blockchain ecosystems may appreciate the ability to move assets seamlessly between different games or external decentralized applications (dApps), creating a more interconnected and expansive gaming experience.

8. Balancing Complexity for Diverse Audiences

User-Selectable Complexity Levels: An effective strategy for catering to both casual gamers and crypto natives is to offer user-selectable complexity levels. Players can choose their preferred level of involvement in the economic aspects of the game, ranging from simplified casual gameplay to advanced strategies for crypto-savvy enthusiasts.

Progressive Learning Paths: Implementing progressive learning paths allows players to gradually explore more complex gameplay mechanics. Casual gamers can start with basic features and gradually unlock additional layers of complexity as they become more familiar with the game and blockchain concepts.

9. Community Building Across Audiences

Inclusive Community Spaces: Creating inclusive community spaces within the game fosters interaction between casual gamers and crypto natives. This inclusive environment allows experienced players to share insights and knowledge with newcomers, promoting a supportive atmosphere that benefits the entire player community.

Collaborative Events and Challenges: Organizing collaborative events and challenges encourages both casual gamers and crypto natives to come together. Shared goals and objectives create opportunities for learning, collaboration, and community-building, bridging the gap between diverse player profiles.

10. Iterative Design Based on User Feedback

Feedback Loops for Continuous Improvement: Implementing feedback loops based on user input is crucial for iterative design. Regularly collecting feedback from both casual gamers and crypto natives allows developers to identify areas for improvement, adjust gameplay mechanics, and refine in-game economic models to better suit the preferences of the player base.

Adapting to Shifting Audience Dynamics: As the play-to-earn gaming landscape evolves, developers must remain adaptable to shifting audience dynamics. Trends in player preferences, blockchain technology advancements, and broader market influences should inform ongoing adjustments to game design, ensuring continued relevance and appeal to diverse player segments.

Balancing the focus between casual gamers and crypto natives is an intricate dance that requires careful consideration of user needs, preferences, and the evolving landscape of play-to-earn gaming. By implementing thoughtful design strategies, play-to-earn games can create engaging experiences that cater to both newcomers and experienced blockchain enthusiasts, fostering a more inclusive and vibrant gaming ecosystem.

Allowing True Ownership of Assets via NFTs

The integration of Non-Fungible Tokens (NFTs) within play-to-earn gaming represents a revolutionary shift in the concept of ownership within virtual environments. This chapter delves into the significance of NFTs, exploring how they enable true ownership of in-game assets, the impact on player experiences, and the broader implications for the play-to-earn gaming landscape.

1. Understanding NFTs and Ownership in Virtual Worlds

Defining Non-Fungible Tokens (NFTs): Non-Fungible Tokens are unique cryptographic assets that represent ownership of distinct items or assets. In the context of play-to-earn gaming, NFTs are used to represent in-game items, characters, and other virtual assets, allowing players to have verifiable ownership on the blockchain.

True Ownership vs. Traditional Models: Traditional gaming models often limit players' ownership rights to in-game assets. With NFTs, true ownership is established through blockchain technology, giving players control over their digital possessions outside the confines of a specific game or platform. This paradigm shift enhances the player's sense of value and permanence associated with their virtual assets.

2. NFTs as Provably Scarce and Unique Digital Assets

Scarcity and Rarity in Digital Form: NFTs introduce scarcity and rarity to the digital realm. Each NFT is unique and cannot be replicated, providing players with the opportunity to own items with intrinsic value and scarcity. This aspect mirrors the concept of rare and valuable physical collectibles but in a digital format.

Verifiable Authenticity and Provenance: Blockchain's transparency ensures the verifiable authenticity and provenance of NFTs. Players can trace the origin and ownership history of their in-game assets, establishing a transparent and immutable record that enhances the perceived value of these digital items.

3. Transforming Digital Assets into Real-World Value

Monetization Beyond the Game: NFTs empower players to monetize their in-game assets beyond the confines of the game environment. Players can sell, trade, or leverage their NFTs in external marketplaces, creating real-world value from their virtual achievements. This dynamic transforms gaming from a leisure activity into a potential source of income.

Cross-Platform Asset Utilization: The true ownership facilitated by NFTs allows players to utilize their assets across different games and platforms. This cross-platform interoperability enhances the versatility and utility of NFT-based assets, encouraging players to explore diverse gaming experiences while retaining ownership of their digital possessions.

4. Impact on Player Engagement and Retention

Emotional Connection to Digital Possessions: The sense of true ownership fosters an emotional connection between players and their in-game assets. Players are more likely to invest time and effort into games where their achievements and possessions hold genuine value, contributing to increased player engagement and longer retention periods.

Player-Generated Content and Creativity: NFTs open the door to player-generated content and creativity. Players can create, customize, and sell their own NFTs, contributing to the richness of the in-game ecosystem. This participatory aspect enhances player satisfaction and the overall vibrancy of the play-to-earn community.

5. Overcoming Challenges of NFT Integration

Scalability Concerns: The integration of NFTs into play-to-earn gaming faces scalability challenges, particularly during periods of high demand. Developers must address issues related to transaction throughput and latency to ensure a seamless and responsive user experience.

Environmental Considerations: The environmental impact of blockchain, especially energy-intensive consensus mechanisms like Proof of Work (PoW), raises concerns. Developers and blockchain networks are exploring eco-friendly alternatives, such as Proof of Stake (PoS), to mitigate the carbon footprint associated with NFT transactions.

6. NFT Standards and Interoperability

Evolution of NFT Standards: NFT standards, such as ERC-721 and ERC-1155 on the Ethereum blockchain, have become widely adopted. The evolution of these standards and the emergence of cross-chain compatibility contribute to a more standardized and interoperable NFT ecosystem, allowing assets to move seamlessly across different blockchains.

Interoperability Challenges and Solutions: Interoperability challenges may arise when players seek to use their NFTs across different gaming platforms. Developers are exploring solutions to enhance interoperability, including cross-chain bridges and standardized protocols, to ensure a fluid experience for players navigating various virtual worlds.

7. NFTs and In-Game Economies

Economic Impact of Tradable Virtual Assets: NFTs contribute to the development of robust in-game economies. Tradable virtual assets enable player-driven markets where the supply and demand for NFTs influence their value. Developers can strategically design economic models that align with player behaviors, fostering a thriving virtual marketplace.

Player-Centric Value Propositions: The integration of NFTs shifts the value proposition of in-game economies to be more player-centric. Players are not only consumers of in-game content but active contributors to the economic ecosystem. This shift enhances player agency and encourages a more participatory approach to the virtual economy.

8. Addressing Concerns About Ownership and Security

Smart Contract Audits and Security Measures: Addressing concerns about ownership and security involves rigorous smart contract audits and the implementation of robust security measures. Ensuring the integrity of the underlying blockchain code and adopting best practices for securing NFTs are essential to building trust among players regarding the ownership of their digital assets.

Educating Players on Security Practices: Educating players on security practices, such as the importance of securing private keys and using reputable wallets, is crucial. By fostering a culture of security awareness, developers contribute to a safer environment for players to enjoy true ownership of their NFT-based assets.

9. Future Innovations in NFT Integration

Dynamic NFT Functionality: The future of NFT integration involves exploring dynamic functionality beyond static ownership. Developers can implement NFTs with programmable features, allowing assets to evolve, change, or gain new abilities over time. This dynamic aspect adds a layer of unpredictability and excitement to the concept of true ownership.

Augmented Reality (AR) and Virtual Reality (VR) Enhancements: Incorporating augmented reality (AR) and virtual reality (VR) enhancements to NFTs can further blur the lines between the virtual and physical worlds. Players may experience their NFT-based assets in real-world environments, enhancing the immersive nature of true ownership.

10. Community Perspectives and Testimonials

Player Testimonials on NFT Ownership: Including player testimonials provides a firsthand perspective on the impact of NFT ownership. Stories of players benefiting financially, emotionally connecting with their digital assets, or contributing to the play-to-earn ecosystem offer valuable insights into the real-world implications of true ownership facilitated by NFTs.

Community Forums and Discussions: Engaging players in community forums and discussions allows developers to gather feedback on the implementation of NFTs. Understanding player experiences, concerns, and suggestions helps refine the integration of true ownership within play-to-earn gaming, ensuring that NFTs align with the desires of the player community.

In conclusion, the integration of NFTs and the facilitation of true ownership represent a transformative leap in play-to-earn gaming. As developers navigate the challenges and seize the opportunities presented by NFTs, they contribute to a future where players not only enjoy immersive virtual experiences but also wield true ownership over their digital assets, creating a paradigm shift in the relationship between players and the virtual worlds they inhabit.

Creating Vibrant Virtual Worlds and Communities

The development of vibrant virtual worlds and communities is a cornerstone of play-to-earn gaming, shaping the player experience and fostering a sense of belonging within the digital landscape. This chapter explores the strategies, design principles, and community-building initiatives that contribute to the creation of immersive virtual environments and flourishing player communities in the context of play-to-earn gaming.

1. Defining the Essence of Virtual Worlds

Beyond Graphics: Creating vibrant virtual worlds extends beyond stunning graphics. It encompasses the thoughtful design of landscapes, architecture, and environments that captivate players and immerse them in a rich and dynamic setting. From fantastical realms to sci-fi landscapes, the virtual world serves as the canvas for the play-to-earn gaming experience.

Interactive Environments: Interactivity is key to a vibrant virtual world. Environments that respond to player actions, feature dynamic elements, and offer hidden surprises contribute to a sense of exploration and discovery. The goal is to make the virtual world a living, breathing entity that evolves with player engagement.

2. Player-Centric Design for Immersive Experiences

User-Centered Design Principles: A player-centric approach to design involves understanding player preferences, behaviors, and desires. User-centered design principles guide the creation of virtual worlds that resonate with players, ensuring that the overall gaming experience is intuitive, enjoyable, and tailored to the community's collective interests.

Customization and Personalization: Allowing players to customize their in-game surroundings fosters a sense of ownership and personalization. From customizable avatars to player-owned spaces, the ability to shape and personalize the virtual environment strengthens the bond between players and the world they inhabit.

3. Fostering Dynamic and Inclusive Communities

Community as an Integral Component: A vibrant virtual world is incomplete without a thriving community. Developers recognize that community-building is as crucial as world-building. Inclusive spaces where players can interact, collaborate, and share experiences contribute to the overall richness of the play-to-earn ecosystem.

Social Features and Communication Tools: Incorporating social features and robust communication tools within the game infrastructure enhances community engagement. From in-game chat systems to social hubs, these tools facilitate real-time interaction, collaboration, and the formation of social bonds among players.

4. The Role of Player-Generated Content

Empowering Players as Creators: Empowering players to generate content contributes to the vibrancy of virtual worlds. Whether through user-generated quests, custom-designed assets, or player-created events, allowing players to actively contribute to the content ecosystem fosters a sense of co-creation and shared ownership.

Community-Driven Events and Festivals: Organizing community-driven events and festivals within the virtual world brings players together in celebration. From in-game holidays to player-run tournaments, these events create memorable experiences and strengthen the sense of community camaraderie.

5. Balancing Realism and Fantasy

Immersive Realism: While play-to-earn games often explore fantastical themes, incorporating elements of realism can enhance immersion. Attention to detail in the virtual world, realistic physics, and a cohesive design that adheres to an internal logic contribute to the creation of an immersive and believable environment.

Fantasy and Escapism: On the flip side, embracing fantasy allows players to escape the constraints of reality. Unique landscapes, magical elements, and fantastical creatures contribute to a sense of wonder and exploration, providing players with an otherworldly experience within the virtual realm.

6. Incorporating Lore and Storytelling

Building a Compelling Narrative: A well-crafted narrative adds depth to the virtual world. Developing a rich lore, backstory, and ongoing narrative arcs provides players with a sense of purpose and context. The storyline becomes a driving force for exploration and engagement, connecting players to the broader narrative of the play-to-earn universe.

Player-Driven Stories: Allowing players to influence the unfolding narrative creates a dynamic storytelling experience. Player actions, choices, and achievements can shape the course of the virtual world's history, making each player's journey a unique and integral part of the overall narrative tapestry.

7. Challenges and Rewards Within the Virtual World

Balancing Difficulty Levels: Introducing challenges within the virtual world adds a layer of gameplay complexity. Balancing difficulty levels ensures that tasks and quests are engaging without being overly daunting. A well-calibrated challenge-reward system motivates players to explore, strategize, and collaborate to overcome in-game obstacles.

Rewarding Exploration and Creativity: Incentivizing exploration and creativity enhances the player experience. Virtual worlds that reward players for uncovering hidden areas, solving puzzles, or creating unique in-game content contribute to a sense of achievement and encourage players to fully immerse themselves in the digital landscape.

8. Incentivizing Social Interaction

Group Activities and Team Challenges: Designing group activities and team challenges encourages social interaction. From cooperative quests to large-scale raids, creating opportunities for players to collaborate fosters a sense of community and teamwork within the virtual world.

Social Rewards and Recognition: Incentivizing social interactions with rewards and recognition reinforces positive community behaviors. Whether through in-game achievements, leaderboards, or exclusive social perks, acknowledging and celebrating player contributions to the community strengthens social bonds.

9. Moderation and Governance in Virtual Communities

Establishing Community Guidelines: To maintain a positive and inclusive environment, developers establish clear community guidelines. These guidelines outline acceptable behavior, discourage toxicity, and ensure that the virtual community remains a welcoming space for players of all backgrounds.

Community Moderation and Governance Tools: Implementing robust community moderation and governance tools helps maintain order within the virtual world. Features such as reporting mechanisms, moderation teams, and transparent governance structures empower players to actively contribute to the upkeep of a healthy and thriving community.

10. Technological Advancements and Future Possibilities

Integration of Emerging Technologies: The future of vibrant virtual worlds lies in the integration of emerging technologies. From augmented reality (AR) enhancements to blockchain-based innovations, staying at the forefront of technological advancements enables developers to continuously elevate the player experience and the overall vibrancy of the virtual landscape.

Interconnected Metaverse Ecosystems: The concept of interconnected metaverse ecosystems represents the next frontier in play-to-earn gaming. Creating seamless connections between different virtual worlds allows players to traverse diverse landscapes and engage in cross-platform experiences, contributing to a more expansive and interconnected gaming universe.

In conclusion, the creation of vibrant virtual worlds and communities is a multifaceted endeavor that requires a careful balance of design, community-building initiatives, and technological innovation. By prioritizing player engagement, inclusivity, and the cultivation of a dynamic virtual ecosystem, developers contribute to the evolution of play-to-earn gaming as not just a game but a living, breathing digital universe where players can forge their own paths and shape the future of the virtual worlds they inhabit.

Balancing Playability and Earnings Potential

Achieving the delicate equilibrium between playability and earnings potential is a pivotal challenge in the design of play-to-earn games. This chapter explores the intricacies of striking this balance, delving into design considerations, economic models, and player experiences that contribute to a harmonious relationship between enjoyable gameplay and meaningful financial rewards within the play-to-earn ecosystem.

1. Playability as the Foundation

Defining Playability: Playability refers to the ease with which players can engage with and enjoy a game. It encompasses factors such as intuitive controls, engaging mechanics, and an overall user-friendly experience. Prioritizing playability is fundamental to attracting and retaining a diverse player base.

The Importance of Player Enjoyment: An enjoyable gaming experience is the foundation of player retention. Playability ensures that the game is accessible, entertaining, and capable of capturing the player's attention. Whether through captivating narratives, exciting gameplay mechanics, or visually appealing aesthetics, player enjoyment is paramount.

2. Navigating the Complexity of Earnings Potential

Earnings Potential as a Motivator: Earnings potential adds a layer of complexity to play-to-earn games, transforming them from pure entertainment into platforms where players can derive tangible value from their in-game activities. Balancing this financial incentive with playability is crucial to prevent the gamification of work and maintain the essence of gaming as an enjoyable pastime.

The Dual Nature of Play-to-Earn: Play-to-earn games operate on a dual nature – providing entertainment through gameplay while offering the potential for financial gains. Striking the right balance ensures that players are motivated to participate in the economic aspects without compromising the core essence of gaming.

3. Designing Intuitive Economic Models

Clear and Transparent Earning Mechanisms: Intuitive economic models are vital for balancing playability and earnings potential. Players should easily understand how their in-game actions translate into earnings. Clear and transparent earning mechanisms prevent confusion and foster a sense of trust in the economic systems of play-to-earn games.

Alignment with Gameplay Objectives: Economic models should align seamlessly with gameplay objectives. Earnings potential should complement the natural progression of the game, encouraging players to explore, engage, and achieve within the virtual world. The integration of earning opportunities into the fabric of gameplay enhances the overall player experience.

4. The Role of In-Game Currency and Tokens

Utility of In-Game Currency: In-game currencies play a pivotal role in balancing playability and earnings potential. These currencies serve as the medium through which players earn, spend, and trade within the game. Designing a balanced in-game economy ensures that the earning potential of these currencies aligns with player expectations and in-game value.

Integration of Blockchain Tokens: Many play-to-earn games leverage blockchain tokens as a form of value transfer. Integrating blockchain tokens adds a layer of authenticity, allowing players to truly own and trade their in-game assets. The design challenge lies in ensuring that the introduction of blockchain tokens enhances, rather than disrupts, the overall playability of the game.

5. Balancing Grind and Reward

Engaging Grind vs. Monotonous Grind: Balancing the grind is a critical aspect of playability. Engaging grind involves activities that are enjoyable, challenging, and contribute to the player's sense of accomplishment. On the other hand, monotonous grind, where repetitive tasks are the primary source of earnings, can lead to player fatigue and a diminished gaming experience.

Dynamic Rewards and Progression: Implementing dynamic rewards and progression systems mitigates the risk of monotonous grind. Varied tasks, evolving challenges, and a range of rewards keep players engaged. A well-designed progression system ensures that players experience a sense of growth and achievement without falling into repetitive and uninteresting gameplay loops.

6. Player Agency in Economic Decision-Making

Informed Decision-Making: Empowering players with agency in economic decision-making enhances playability. Players should have the autonomy to make informed choices about how they earn, spend, and invest within the game. This level of agency contributes to a more immersive and personalized gaming experience.

Risk and Reward Dynamics: Balancing risk and reward dynamics is crucial in play-to-earn games. Players should be aware of the potential risks associated with certain in-game actions, such as investments or trading decisions. Striking the right balance ensures that the pursuit of earnings is accompanied by strategic decision-making and calculated risks.

7. Preventing Exploitative Gameplay Dynamics

Ethical Design Considerations: Maintaining ethical design considerations is paramount in preventing exploitative gameplay dynamics. Developers must be vigilant against creating systems that encourage unhealthy gaming habits, addiction, or excessive financial risk-taking. Ethical considerations contribute to the long-term sustainability of play-to-earn ecosystems.

Fair Distribution of Rewards: Ensuring a fair distribution of rewards is essential for preventing exploitation. Players should be rewarded based on their contributions and achievements rather than relying on exploitative mechanisms. Fairness in reward distribution builds trust and fosters a positive community culture.

8. Addressing Inflation and Deflation Concerns

Inflationary Pressures: Inflation within the in-game economy can erode the value of in-game assets and currency. Developers must implement measures to address inflationary pressures, such as controlled token issuance or mechanisms that balance the creation and removal of in-game assets.

Deflationary Risks: Conversely, deflationary risks, where the scarcity of assets leads to excessive value accumulation, also pose challenges. Striking a balance between inflation and deflation is crucial for maintaining a stable and sustainable economic model within play-to-earn games.

9. The Influence of External Factors

Market Dynamics and Cryptocurrency Trends: External factors, such as broader market dynamics and cryptocurrency trends, can impact the playability and earnings potential of play-to-earn games. Developers must remain adaptable to changes in market conditions, ensuring that the economic model remains resilient and responsive to external influences.

Regulatory Considerations: The evolving regulatory landscape surrounding cryptocurrencies and virtual assets adds a layer of complexity. Developers must navigate regulatory considerations to ensure compliance and mitigate risks that could impact the playability and earnings potential of their games.

10. Evolving with Player Feedback and Iterative Design

Continuous Iteration Based on Feedback: Playability and earnings potential are not static concepts; they evolve based on player feedback and the ever-changing gaming landscape. Implementing a continuous feedback loop and adopting an iterative design approach allows developers to refine economic models, address player concerns, and adapt to the evolving needs of the player community.

Community Engagement in Design Decisions: Engaging the player community in design decisions is a powerful strategy. Community feedback provides valuable insights into the player experience, helping developers make informed decisions that resonate with the desires and expectations of the community.

In conclusion, the delicate balance between playability and earnings potential is at the heart of successful play-to-earn game design. By carefully considering the interplay between enjoyable gameplay, transparent economic models, and player agency, developers can create immersive gaming experiences that not only captivate players but also offer meaningful financial incentives within the dynamic and evolving world of play-to-earn gaming.

Chapter 6 - Guilds and the Player Ecosystem
The Role and Operations of Scholar and Player Guilds

Scholar and player guilds play a pivotal role in shaping the player ecosystem within play-to-earn gaming. This chapter explores the intricate dynamics, functions, and impact of both scholar and player guilds, shedding light on how these organizational structures contribute to the overall success, growth, and inclusivity of play-to-earn gaming communities.

1. Understanding Scholar Guilds

Definition and Purpose: Scholar guilds are organizational structures within play-to-earn games designed to facilitate mentorship and guidance. Scholars, experienced players or experts in the game, take on the role of mentors, guiding newer or less-experienced players, known as scholars, in navigating the complexities of the game. The primary purpose is to accelerate the learning curve for scholars and provide a supportive environment for their growth.

Recruitment and Onboarding: Scholar guilds actively recruit scholars and scholars-in-training. The onboarding process involves introducing new scholars to the game mechanics, strategies, and the guild's specific rules and expectations. This mentorship model helps scholars integrate into the broader play-to-earn community more seamlessly.

2. Operations of Scholar Guilds

Structured Mentorship Programs: Organized mentorship programs are a hallmark of scholar guilds. These programs often include one-on-one mentorship sessions, group activities, and workshops designed to enhance the skills and knowledge of scholars. Structured mentorship ensures that scholars receive comprehensive guidance tailored to their individual needs.

Resource Sharing and Collaboration: Scholar guilds foster a collaborative environment where resources, strategies, and insights are shared among members. This collective knowledge pool enables scholars to overcome challenges, optimize their in-game performance, and stay informed about the evolving dynamics of play-to-earn games.

3. The Impact of Scholar Guilds

Empowering New Entrants: Scholar guilds play a crucial role in empowering new entrants to play-to-earn gaming. By providing access to experienced mentors, these guilds enable scholars to navigate the learning curve more efficiently, empowering them to make informed decisions and contribute meaningfully to the play-to-earn ecosystem.

Community Building and Camaraderie: The mentorship and collaborative nature of scholar guilds contribute to the building of a strong sense of community and camaraderie. Scholars often form lasting bonds with their mentors and fellow guild members, creating a supportive network that extends beyond the virtual confines of the game.

4. Understanding Player Guilds

Definition and Purpose: Player guilds, also known as gaming clans or teams, are communities formed by players who share common interests, goals, or affiliations within a play-to-earn game. These guilds operate beyond the mentorship model, focusing on collective gameplay, competition, and community-building among players with varying levels of experience.

Recruitment and Guild Affiliation: Players join guilds based on shared objectives, playstyles, or affiliations. Guilds may be open for all players or require an application process to ensure alignment with the guild's values and goals. Affiliation with a player guild often involves representing the guild in in-game activities and competitions.

5. Operations of Player Guilds

Collaborative Gameplay and Strategies: Player guilds emphasize collaborative gameplay, with members working together to achieve common objectives. Guilds often develop specific strategies, tactics, and playstyles that align with their goals, fostering a sense of unity and coordination among members during in-game activities.

Internal Structures and Leadership: Player guilds typically have internal structures, including leadership roles and hierarchies. Guild leaders and officers coordinate activities, enforce guild rules, and serve as points of contact for members. Establishing clear leadership structures helps maintain order and organization within the guild.

6. The Impact of Player Guilds

Competitive Edge and Achievements: Player guilds contribute to the competitive landscape of play-to-earn gaming. Guilds often participate in tournaments, competitions, and in-game events, showcasing their collective skills and strategies. The achievements of guild members, both as individuals and as part of the guild, enhance the overall reputation and standing of the guild within the broader gaming community.

Community Engagement and Social Interaction: Player guilds foster community engagement and social interaction among members. Beyond the shared pursuit of in-game goals, guilds often organize social events, discussions, and community-building initiatives. This social dimension enhances the overall gaming experience, transforming it into a dynamic and interactive community.

7. Synergy Between Scholar and Player Guilds

Collaboration and Knowledge Exchange: In some play-to-earn ecosystems, a synergistic relationship exists between scholar and player guilds. Scholar guilds contribute by nurturing new talent and guiding players through their initial experiences, while player guilds benefit from a pool of well-trained and informed players. Collaboration and knowledge exchange between these guild types create a balanced and inclusive player ecosystem.

Creating Pathways for Growth: The interaction between scholar and player guilds creates pathways for growth within the play-to-earn community. Scholars, after gaining experience and proficiency, may transition to player guilds, bringing their knowledge and mentorship skills to a more competitive and collaborative gaming environment.

8. Challenges and Controversies

Controversies Around Exploitation: The dynamic between scholars and player guilds can sometimes lead to controversies, particularly around the potential exploitation of scholar programs. Concerns may arise regarding the fair treatment of scholars, the balance of benefits, and the ethical considerations of mentorship programs within the context of play-to-earn gaming.

Addressing Power Imbalances: To ensure a healthy ecosystem, developers and guild leaders must address power imbalances that may emerge within guild structures. Strategies to mitigate these imbalances include transparent communication, fair distribution of rewards, and the establishment of clear guidelines for mentorship programs.

9. Case Studies and Success Stories

Showcasing Positive Guild Dynamics: Highlighting case studies and success stories from both scholar and player guilds offers insights into positive guild dynamics. These narratives provide examples of effective mentorship, collaborative gameplay, and community-building initiatives, serving as inspiration for other guilds within the play-to-earn ecosystem.

10. Future Trends and Evolution of Guild Dynamics

Integration of Blockchain and NFTs: The integration of blockchain and NFTs into guild dynamics represents a potential future trend. Blockchain technology can enhance transparency in guild operations, and NFTs may be used to represent guild affiliations, achievements, or unique in-game assets tied to guild memberships.

Evolving Models for Inclusivity: As play-to-earn gaming continues to evolve, guild dynamics may adapt to foster greater inclusivity. Developers and guild leaders may explore innovative models that encourage collaboration between scholars and players, creating environments where both newcomers and seasoned players can thrive.

In conclusion, scholar and player guilds are integral components of the play-to-earn ecosystem, contributing to the growth, competitiveness, and sense of community within these virtual worlds. By understanding the distinct roles, operations, and impacts of these guild structures, players, developers, and the broader gaming community can actively participate in and shape the vibrant and dynamic landscape of play-to-earn gaming.

Providing Access and Education to New Crypto Users

In the dynamic landscape of play-to-earn gaming, one of the crucial roles that guilds play is in providing access and education to new crypto users. This chapter explores the multifaceted aspects of how guilds serve as gateways for individuals entering the world of cryptocurrencies, fostering an environment of learning, inclusivity, and empowerment within the play-to-earn ecosystem.

1. Onboarding New Crypto Users

Introduction to Cryptocurrencies: Guilds act as entry points for individuals unfamiliar with cryptocurrencies. They offer comprehensive onboarding processes that introduce new users to the basics of blockchain technology, digital wallets, and the use of cryptocurrencies within the play-to-earn ecosystem. This foundational knowledge is crucial for empowering users to navigate the crypto space confidently.

Creating User-Friendly Onboarding Experiences: Guilds prioritize creating user-friendly onboarding experiences to minimize barriers to entry. This involves developing intuitive guides, tutorials, and step-by-step instructions for setting up crypto wallets, understanding transaction processes, and interacting with blockchain-based assets.

2. Education on Blockchain Technology

Understanding Blockchain Principles: Guilds serve as educational hubs, helping new users grasp the principles of blockchain technology. This includes explaining decentralized ledgers, smart contracts, and the security features that underpin blockchain networks. A solid understanding of these fundamentals equips users to engage more effectively in the play-to-earn ecosystem.

Exploring Decentralized Finance (DeFi): As part of the education process, guilds introduce users to decentralized finance (DeFi) concepts. This includes insights into lending, staking, and yield farming within the crypto space. DeFi education empowers users to explore additional opportunities beyond gaming, broadening their participation in the broader crypto economy.

3. Navigating Crypto Wallets and Exchanges

Choosing and Using Wallets: Navigating the variety of crypto wallets can be overwhelming for newcomers. Guilds guide users in choosing wallets based on security features, user-friendliness, and compatibility with the specific play-to-earn game. Tutorials on setting up, securing, and using wallets ensure a seamless entry into the crypto ecosystem.

Introduction to Crypto Exchanges: Understanding how to use crypto exchanges is a vital aspect of crypto education. Guilds provide guidance on selecting reputable exchanges, creating accounts, and executing trades. This knowledge is essential for users looking to convert, trade, or acquire cryptocurrencies to enhance their play-to-earn gaming experience.

4. Token Acquisition and Management

Earning and Acquiring Tokens: Guilds educate users on various methods of earning and acquiring in-game tokens. This includes participation in game activities, completing quests, and understanding the economic models of play-to-earn games. Users learn how to accumulate tokens and leverage them within the gaming ecosystem.

Security and Custody of Tokens: Ensuring the security and proper custody of tokens is paramount. Guilds provide education on best practices for securing private keys, implementing two-factor authentication, and using hardware wallets. This knowledge safeguards users against potential security risks associated with token ownership.

5. Community-Led Learning Initiatives

Interactive Workshops and Webinars: Guilds organize interactive workshops and webinars led by experienced members or industry experts. These sessions cover a range of topics, from advanced blockchain concepts to practical tips for navigating the crypto space. Community-led learning initiatives create a collaborative environment where users can actively engage and ask questions.

Knowledge Sharing Platforms: Guilds establish knowledge-sharing platforms such as forums, chat groups, and online communities. These spaces allow users to seek advice, share experiences, and learn from one another. The community-driven nature of these platforms fosters a culture of continuous learning within the guild and the broader play-to-earn community.

6. Inclusive Practices for Diverse Audiences

Localized Education and Support: Recognizing the global nature of play-to-earn gaming, guilds adopt localized approaches to education. This includes providing educational content in multiple languages, understanding cultural nuances, and tailoring support services to cater to diverse audiences. Inclusivity ensures that players from various backgrounds feel welcome and supported.

Accessibility for Players with Different Backgrounds: Guilds actively promote accessibility by considering the diverse backgrounds of their user base. This involves addressing the needs of players with varying levels of technical expertise, financial literacy, and cultural familiarity with gaming and cryptocurrencies. Creating a welcoming and inclusive environment encourages broader participation.

7. Mentorship Programs for New Crypto Users

Establishing Mentorship Structures: Guilds often implement mentorship programs where experienced members guide new crypto users. This one-on-one mentorship provides personalized support, addressing the specific needs and questions of individuals as they navigate the complexities of cryptocurrencies. Mentorship fosters a sense of community and mutual assistance.

Encouraging Peer-to-Peer Support: In addition to formal mentorship programs, guilds encourage peer-to-peer support within the community. Experienced users willingly share their knowledge with newcomers, creating a collaborative atmosphere where individuals feel comfortable seeking guidance from their peers.

8. Challenges and Solutions in Crypto Education

Addressing Information Overload: The crypto space can be overwhelming due to the abundance of information. Guilds proactively address information overload by curating and presenting essential knowledge in a structured manner. Clear pathways for learning help users focus on key concepts before delving into more advanced topics.

Navigating Regulatory Complexity: Educating users about the regulatory landscape is crucial. Guilds provide insights into the legal aspects of cryptocurrency use, helping users understand compliance requirements and navigate the evolving regulatory environment. This knowledge safeguards users and ensures responsible participation.

9. Real-World Application of Crypto Knowledge

Translating Knowledge into Practical Actions: Guilds emphasize the practical application of crypto knowledge within the play-to-earn ecosystem. This includes guiding users on earning, spending, and managing their crypto assets within the gaming environment. The real-world application of knowledge enhances the user experience and reinforces the value of crypto education.

10. Evolution of Education in Guild Dynamics

Adapting to Technological Advances: As the crypto and gaming landscapes evolve, guilds remain adaptable to technological advances. This includes incorporating innovations such as blockchain integrations, interactive educational platforms, and immersive learning experiences. Adapting to technological changes ensures that education within guilds remains relevant and engaging.

Building Bridges to Broader Cryptocurrency Adoption: Guilds play a pivotal role in building bridges to broader cryptocurrency adoption beyond the play-to-earn gaming sphere. By educating users on the fundamentals of cryptocurrencies and blockchain technology, guilds contribute to the larger goal of fostering mainstream acceptance and understanding of these transformative technologies.

In conclusion, guilds act as catalysts for providing access and education to new crypto users, playing a vital role in demystifying the complexities of the crypto space. By focusing on inclusivity, mentorship, and community-led learning initiatives, guilds contribute to the growth and sustainability of play-to-earn gaming while empowering individuals to navigate the exciting world of cryptocurrencies.

Economics and Profit-Sharing Models Between Guilds and Players

In the intricate ecosystem of play-to-earn gaming, the relationship between guilds and players extends beyond gameplay and community dynamics to encompass economic aspects. This chapter delves into the nuanced economics of guilds, exploring the profit-sharing models that define the collaboration between guilds and players. From in-game earnings to external revenue streams, understanding these economic frameworks is essential for comprehending the symbiotic relationship that underpins the success of guilds within the play-to-earn landscape.

1. In-Game Earnings and Revenue Generation

Guilds as Economic Hubs: Guilds serve as economic hubs within play-to-earn ecosystems, actively participating in in-game economies. Players affiliated with guilds often benefit from shared resources, cooperative gameplay, and enhanced opportunities for earning in-game assets. This section examines the dynamics of in-game earnings within guilds and how collective efforts contribute to economic prosperity.

Pooling In-Game Resources: Guilds often employ pooling mechanisms where in-game resources, such as tokens, items, or virtual assets, are collectively owned or managed by the guild. The pooling of resources enhances the overall economic strength of the guild and allows for strategic decision-making regarding resource allocation and utilization.

2. Guild Governance and Decision-Making

Transparent Governance Structures: Economic interactions within guilds are governed by transparent structures that outline decision-making processes, resource distribution, and profit-sharing mechanisms. This transparency ensures that all members have visibility into the guild's economic activities, fostering trust and accountability within the community.

Democratic Decision-Making: Many guilds adopt democratic decision-making models where members collectively contribute to economic decisions. This may include voting on resource allocation, investment strategies, and the distribution of profits. Democratic governance models empower players to actively participate in shaping the economic direction of the guild.

3. Revenue Streams Beyond In-Game Earnings

External Partnerships and Collaborations: Guilds explore external partnerships and collaborations as a means of diversifying their revenue streams. This involves forging alliances with gaming platforms, sponsors, and other entities interested in the play-to-earn ecosystem. The revenue generated from these collaborations contributes to the overall economic health of the guild.

Participation in Play-to-Earn Platforms: Some guilds actively engage with external play-to-earn platforms that facilitate cross-game asset trading or investment opportunities. This participation opens up new avenues for revenue generation, allowing guilds to leverage their collective assets and expertise in broader play-to-earn ecosystems.

4. Profit-Sharing Models Between Guilds and Players

Equitable Distribution of In-Game Profits: Guilds establish profit-sharing models that ensure an equitable distribution of in-game profits among members. This includes earnings from quests, competitions, and other in-game activities. Examining these models provides insights into how guilds balance individual contributions with collective benefits, fostering a sense of fairness and cooperation.

Performance-Based Rewards: Guilds often implement performance-based reward systems, where players who contribute significantly to the guild's success receive additional incentives. This can include a share of the guild's earnings, exclusive in-game assets, or other tangible rewards. Performance-based models encourage active participation and excellence within the guild.

5. Investment Strategies and Guild Development

Strategic Investments in In-Game Assets: Guilds strategically invest in in-game assets, anticipating potential appreciation or increased demand. This economic foresight allows guilds to optimize their resource allocation, maximize returns, and enhance the overall wealth of the guild and its members.

Guild Development Initiatives: Economic prosperity enables guilds to undertake development initiatives that benefit the entire community. This may include funding for events, infrastructure within the game, or educational programs. Examining these initiatives provides insights into how economic success translates into broader community development.

6. Challenges and Risk Mitigation

Risks Associated with In-Game Economies: The economic landscape of play-to-earn gaming is not without risks. Guilds face challenges related to market volatility, changes in in-game economies, and the potential devaluation of virtual assets. Exploring these risks and effective risk mitigation strategies is crucial for the sustainability of guild-based economies.

Ensuring Fairness and Inclusivity: One challenge lies in ensuring that profit-sharing models are fair and inclusive. Guilds must address issues of transparency, equal opportunities for earning, and the prevention of any form of economic exploitation. Implementing mechanisms that promote fairness and inclusivity strengthens the economic fabric of the guild.

7. Case Studies and Success Stories

Highlighting Economic Success within Guilds: Case studies and success stories offer valuable insights into guilds that have achieved notable economic success. Analyzing these cases sheds light on effective economic strategies, innovative profit-sharing models, and the factors that contribute to sustained economic prosperity within play-to-earn guilds.

8. Future Trends in Guild Economics

Integration of Blockchain and Smart Contracts: The integration of blockchain technology and smart contracts presents future trends in guild economics. Blockchain can enhance transparency in economic transactions, and smart contracts can automate profit-sharing mechanisms. Exploring these trends provides a glimpse into the potential evolution of guild economics.

Exploration of Decentralized Autonomous Organizations (DAOs): Some guilds may explore the concept of decentralized autonomous organizations (DAOs) to govern economic activities. DAOs utilize blockchain technology to enable decentralized decision-making and transparent governance, potentially revolutionizing how economic interactions occur within play-to-earn guilds.

9. Community Feedback and Iterative Economic Design

Continuous Iteration Based on Economic Feedback: Economic models within guilds are subject to continuous iteration based on community feedback. Guilds actively seek input from members to refine profit-sharing models, address economic challenges, and adapt to the evolving dynamics of play-to-earn gaming. This iterative approach ensures that economic structures align with the needs and expectations of the community.

10. Conclusion: Balancing Economic Success and Community Harmony

Striking a Balance Between Economic Prosperity and Community Harmony: In conclusion, the intricate dance between guild economics and community harmony is essential for the sustained success of play-to-earn guilds. Striking a balance between economic prosperity and the well-being of the community ensures that guilds remain vibrant, cooperative spaces where players can thrive both individually and collectively within the dynamic world of play-to-earn gaming.

Controversies Around Potential Exploitation

Within the intricate dynamics of play-to-earn gaming and guild ecosystems, controversies around potential exploitation have surfaced, raising ethical concerns and challenging the perceived fairness of these virtual economies. This chapter explores the multifaceted controversies surrounding potential exploitation within guilds, addressing issues such as power imbalances, unfair distribution of resources, and ethical considerations in the play-to-earn landscape.

1. Power Dynamics and Exploitative Practices

Understanding Power Imbalances: Controversies often arise from power imbalances within guilds, where certain players or entities hold disproportionate influence over economic decisions. This section examines instances of exploitative practices stemming from centralized power structures within guilds and their impact on the broader player ecosystem.

Economic Exploitation of Less Experienced Players: Some controversies revolve around the economic exploitation of less experienced players by more seasoned or influential members. This may involve unequal profit-sharing, resource allocation, or the manipulation of in-game economies to the disadvantage of novice players. Analyzing these instances sheds light on the need for ethical guidelines within guilds.

2. Unfair Distribution of In-Game Resources

Hoarding and Monopolization: Controversies can emerge when certain guild members engage in hoarding or monopolizing in-game resources, limiting access for others. Examining these practices illuminates the challenges associated with resource distribution within guilds and the potential impact on the overall player experience.

Manipulation of In-Game Economies: Instances of exploitation may involve the manipulation of in-game economies for personal gain. This could include artificially inflating the value of certain assets, controlling rare items, or engaging in practices that undermine the fair distribution of in-game resources. Analyzing these controversies highlights the delicate balance between individual and collective interests.

3. Questionable Guild Recruitment and Retention Practices

Coercive Recruitment Tactics: Some guilds face criticism for employing coercive or manipulative tactics to recruit and retain members. This may involve promises of significant earnings, exclusive benefits, or misleading information about the guild's economic practices. Evaluating these controversies raises questions about the ethical boundaries of guild recruitment.

Retention Through Economic Dependency: Controversies may arise when guilds intentionally create economic dependencies, making it challenging for players to leave without significant losses. This section explores cases where players feel trapped within guilds due to economic ties, raising ethical concerns about the autonomy of players within these virtual communities.

4. Ethical Considerations in Guild Governance

Transparency and Accountability: Controversies often stem from a lack of transparency and accountability in guild governance. This includes opaque decision-making processes, undisclosed economic practices, and insufficient mechanisms for members to voice concerns. Examining these ethical considerations underscores the importance of clear and ethical guild governance.

Informed Consent and Education: Addressing controversies requires a focus on informed consent and education within guilds. Ethical guilds prioritize educating members about economic practices, potential risks, and the implications of certain decisions. Ensuring that members make informed choices contributes to a more ethical and responsible play-to-earn environment.

5. The Role of Technology and Blockchain

Blockchain's Potential to Address Exploitation: The integration of blockchain technology offers potential solutions to controversies surrounding exploitation. This section explores how blockchain can enhance transparency, decentralize decision-making, and provide immutable records of economic transactions, thereby mitigating certain forms of exploitation within guilds.

Smart Contracts for Fair Profit-Sharing: Smart contracts, powered by blockchain, can be employed to automate and enforce fair profit-sharing models. This technology has the potential to create trustless systems that ensure equitable distribution of earnings among guild members, reducing the likelihood of exploitative practices.

6. Impact on Community Trust and Reputation

Community Backlash and Trust Erosion: Controversies around potential exploitation can lead to community backlash and erosion of trust within guilds. This section examines the consequences of exploitative practices on a guild's reputation, member morale, and overall community cohesion. Understanding these impacts is crucial for guilds seeking long-term sustainability.

Rebuilding Trust Through Ethical Practices: Ethical guilds actively work to rebuild trust by implementing transparent economic practices, addressing past controversies, and fostering a culture of inclusivity. Examining successful strategies for rebuilding trust provides valuable insights for guilds navigating the aftermath of exploitative controversies.

7. Legal and Regulatory Considerations

Navigating Legal and Regulatory Challenges: Controversies around potential exploitation may prompt legal and regulatory scrutiny. This section explores the evolving legal landscape of play-to-earn gaming, examining how guilds navigate potential legal challenges related to exploitative practices and the broader implications for the industry.

The Role of Self-Regulation: Ethical guilds may engage in self-regulation to proactively address potential exploitation and avoid legal pitfalls. This involves establishing internal codes of conduct, ethical guidelines, and mechanisms for addressing disputes. Exploring the role of self-regulation sheds light on the proactive measures guilds can take to uphold ethical standards.

8. Community-Led Initiatives for Ethical Guilds

Empowering Players to Advocate for Ethical Practices: Community-led initiatives play a pivotal role in advocating for ethical practices within guilds. This section explores how players can come together to promote transparency, ethical decision-making, and fair economic practices. Empowering players to actively shape the ethical landscape of guilds contributes to a more resilient and ethical play-to-earn ecosystem.

Creating Ethical Guild Certifications: Inspired by real-world certifications, community-led initiatives may propose the creation of ethical guild certifications. These certifications could be awarded to guilds that meet specific ethical criteria, signaling to players that these guilds adhere to transparent and fair economic practices.

9. Conclusion: Navigating Ethical Challenges for Sustainable Play-to-Earn Ecosystems

Balancing Economic Growth and Ethical Integrity: In conclusion, the controversies surrounding potential exploitation underscore the delicate balance between economic growth and ethical integrity within play-to-earn guilds. Examining these controversies provides valuable lessons for guilds, players, and industry stakeholders seeking to cultivate sustainable and ethical play-to-earn ecosystems. Addressing these challenges collectively contributes to the maturation and longevity of the play-to-earn gaming phenomenon.

How Guilds Contribute to Ecosystem Growth

In the expansive landscape of play-to-earn gaming, guilds emerge as pivotal players not only in the virtual realms of gameplay but also in shaping the broader ecosystem. This chapter delves into the multifaceted ways in which guilds contribute to the growth of the play-to-earn ecosystem. From fostering community engagement to driving innovation and influencing economic dynamics, guilds play a central role in shaping the evolution and expansion of the vibrant play-to-earn gaming phenomenon.

1. Community Building and Engagement

Formation of Virtual Communities: Guilds act as the building blocks of virtual communities within play-to-earn games. This section explores how guilds foster a sense of belonging, camaraderie, and shared goals among players. Examining the social dynamics within guilds sheds light on their role in creating vibrant and engaged player communities.

Community Events and Initiatives: Guilds organize and participate in a myriad of community events, from in-game challenges to real-world meet-ups. These initiatives contribute to the overall ecosystem growth by enhancing player interaction, strengthening relationships, and creating a sense of excitement and unity within the broader play-to-earn community.

2. Knowledge Sharing and Education

Guidance for New Players: Guilds play a crucial role in guiding and educating new players entering the play-to-earn space. This involves sharing insights into game mechanics, economic dynamics, and the overall play-to-earn ecosystem. Examining how guilds contribute to the education of new players sheds light on their role in lowering entry barriers and expanding the player base.

Interactive Learning Platforms: Some guilds establish interactive learning platforms, including tutorials, workshops, and webinars. These platforms serve as hubs for knowledge exchange, empowering players with the skills and information needed to navigate the complexities of play-to-earn gaming. Analyzing the effectiveness of these initiatives provides insights into how guilds contribute to ecosystem growth through education.

3. Economic Impact and Wealth Distribution

Pooling and Distributing Resources: Guilds actively contribute to the growth of the play-to-earn ecosystem by pooling and distributing in-game resources. This includes tokens, assets, and other valuable items that guild members collectively manage. Examining the economic impact of guilds provides insights into how resource pooling contributes to overall ecosystem prosperity.

Investments and Economic Initiatives: Some guilds venture into economic initiatives, such as strategic investments or collaborative projects. These endeavors contribute to the overall economic vitality of the play-to-earn ecosystem. Analyzing how guilds navigate economic opportunities sheds light on their role as catalysts for financial innovation within the gaming space.

4. Innovation in Gameplay and Strategies

Development of Innovative Gameplay Mechanics: Guilds often drive innovation in gameplay mechanics by experimenting with new strategies, tactics, and collaborative approaches. This section explores how guilds contribute to the evolution of game dynamics, enhancing the overall gaming experience and attracting a diverse player base.

Exploration of New Game Formats: Some guilds actively explore and promote new game formats, contributing to the diversification of the play-to-earn gaming landscape. This may involve participation in beta testing, collaboration with game developers, or the creation of custom game modes. Examining these initiatives provides insights into how guilds influence the trajectory of play-to-earn gaming.

5. Fostering Entrepreneurship and Creativity

Support for Player-Driven Initiatives: Guilds often provide support and resources for player-driven initiatives, fostering entrepreneurship within the play-to-earn ecosystem. This includes the development of in-game businesses, content creation, and other creative endeavors. Analyzing the role of guilds in fostering entrepreneurship sheds light on their contribution to a dynamic and innovative gaming environment.

Encouraging Creative Expression: Some guilds actively encourage creative expression among their members, from in-game content creation to the development of external projects. This not only enhances the player experience but also contributes to the overall richness of the play-to-earn ecosystem. Exploring the creative initiatives driven by guilds provides insights into their role as incubators of innovation.

6. Promotion of Inclusivity and Diversity

Inclusive Recruitment Practices: Guilds contribute to ecosystem growth by adopting inclusive recruitment practices, welcoming players from diverse backgrounds and skill levels. This section examines how guilds actively work to create environments that embrace diversity, fostering a sense of inclusivity within the play-to-earn gaming community.

Representation in Gaming: Some guilds take strides to promote representation within the gaming space, ensuring that players from different demographics feel seen and heard. This involves initiatives such as highlighting diverse player stories, supporting underrepresented groups, and actively working towards a more inclusive gaming landscape.

7. Collaboration with Game Developers and Platforms

Engagement with Game Developers: Guilds often engage with game developers, providing valuable feedback, participating in beta testing, and contributing to the improvement of game features. Examining how guilds collaborate with developers provides insights into the symbiotic relationship between player communities and the creators of play-to-earn games.

Participation in Play-to-Earn Platforms: Some guilds actively participate in external play-to-earn platforms, contributing to the broader ecosystem beyond individual games. This involvement may include cross-game trading, investment opportunities, or partnerships with external platforms. Analyzing the role of guilds in these platforms provides a comprehensive view of their impact on ecosystem growth.

8. Economic Partnerships and Alliances

Alliances Between Guilds: Guilds form alliances to leverage collective strengths, share resources, and collaborate on shared goals. This section explores how inter-guild alliances contribute to the growth of the play-to-earn ecosystem by fostering cooperation, creating economic synergies, and enhancing the overall stability of player communities.

Partnerships with External Entities: Guilds may forge partnerships with external entities, including gaming organizations, brands, and even traditional financial institutions. These partnerships contribute to the integration of play-to-earn gaming into the broader cultural and economic landscape. Examining these alliances provides insights into how guilds act as bridges between the gaming world and external stakeholders.

9. Navigating Challenges and Adapting to Change

Adapting to Shifting Economic Landscapes: Guilds contribute to ecosystem growth by demonstrating adaptability in the face of shifting economic landscapes. This involves navigating challenges such as market volatility, changes in game mechanics, and evolving player preferences. Analyzing how guilds adapt to change provides insights into their resilience and capacity to drive sustained ecosystem growth.

Addressing Economic Inequities: Some guilds actively address economic inequities within the play-to-earn ecosystem. This may involve implementing fair profit-sharing models, advocating for ethical practices, and working towards a more inclusive distribution of resources. Examining these initiatives sheds light on how guilds contribute to the mitigation of economic challenges.

10. Conclusion: Guilds as Catalysts for Play-to-Earn Ecosystem Evolution

Sustaining Ecosystem Evolution Through Guild Contributions: In conclusion, guilds stand as dynamic catalysts for the evolution and growth of the play-to-earn gaming ecosystem. Their multifaceted contributions, from community building to economic innovation, shape the landscape in which players engage and thrive. Understanding the role of guilds in fostering ecosystem growth provides valuable insights into the ongoing maturation and diversification of play-to-earn gaming.

Chapter 7 - Real-World Impacts
Socio-Economic Influence in Developing Countries like the Philippines

In the intersection of play-to-earn gaming and real-world impact, the socio-economic influence of these virtual economies extends far beyond the digital realm, notably in developing countries such as the Philippines. This chapter explores the intricate dynamics of how play-to-earn gaming has shaped and influenced socio-economic landscapes, providing opportunities, challenges, and unique experiences for individuals and communities in the Philippines.

Understanding the Philippines Gaming Culture and Landscape

- Historical Context of Gaming: The Philippines has a rich history of gaming culture, from traditional games to the rapid adoption of digital gaming in recent years. Examining the historical context provides insights into the foundational elements that contribute to the country's avid interest in play-to-earn gaming.

- Rise of Internet Connectivity: The proliferation of internet connectivity in the Philippines has played a pivotal role in the growth of online gaming communities. This section explores how increased access to the internet has democratized participation in play-to-earn games, creating new economic opportunities for players.

Impact on Livelihoods and Economic Empowerment

- Earning Opportunities for Filipino Players: Play-to-earn games, particularly popular titles like Axie Infinity, have provided Filipinos with tangible opportunities to earn a livelihood through gaming. Examining the experiences of players sheds light on how in-game activities translate into real-world income, contributing to economic empowerment.

- Addressing Unemployment Challenges: The Philippines faces persistent challenges related to unemployment, particularly among the youth. Play-to-earn gaming has emerged as a viable alternative for income generation, offering a potential solution to address unemployment issues. This section explores the role of play-to-earn in mitigating economic challenges.

Challenges and Ethical Considerations

- Balancing Economic Gains and Well-Being: While play-to-earn gaming presents economic opportunities, it also raises ethical considerations. This section examines the challenges associated with balancing economic gains with the well-being of players, including issues related to burnout, addiction, and the impact on mental health.

- Ensuring Fairness and Inclusivity: The socio-economic impact of play-to-earn gaming in the Philippines includes addressing questions of fairness and inclusivity. Analyzing how different players, including newcomers and seasoned participants, experience economic opportunities sheds light on the importance of creating an inclusive gaming ecosystem.

Cultural Shifts and Community Dynamics

- Cultural Perception of Gaming: Play-to-earn gaming has influenced the cultural perception of gaming in the Philippines. This section explores how gaming is increasingly recognized as a legitimate and viable pursuit, challenging traditional views and contributing to a cultural shift in how Filipinos perceive the value of gaming activities.

- Formation of Gaming Communities: The rise of play-to-earn has led to the formation of vibrant gaming communities in the Philippines. Examining the dynamics of these communities provides insights into how they contribute to social cohesion, shared identity, and the overall cultural fabric in the context of play-to-earn gaming.

Educational Impacts and Skill Development

- Learning Opportunities Through Gaming: Play-to-earn gaming presents unique learning opportunities for Filipino players, ranging from economic principles to strategic thinking. This section explores the educational impact of play-to-earn, examining how players acquire valuable skills through their gaming experiences.

- Skill Transferability to Real-world Contexts: Beyond in-game skills, play-to-earn gaming fosters the development of transferable skills with real-world applications. Analyzing how players leverage skills acquired in the virtual space in educational, professional, and entrepreneurial pursuits highlights the broader impact on skill development.

Government and Regulatory Responses

- Recognition and Regulation: Governments in developing countries, including the Philippines, are increasingly recognizing the economic significance of play-to-earn gaming. This section explores regulatory responses, examining how authorities are navigating the need for recognition and regulation to ensure player protection and fair economic practices.

- Opportunities for Collaboration: Collaboration between the government and the gaming industry presents opportunities for fostering a conducive environment for play-to-earn activities. Examining successful collaborative initiatives sheds light on the potential for synergy between regulatory bodies and gaming stakeholders.

Economic Redistribution and Financial Inclusion

- Redistribution of Wealth: Play-to-earn gaming has the potential to contribute to economic redistribution by providing income-generating opportunities to a broader demographic. This section explores how wealth generated within virtual economies can have a positive impact on financial inclusivity in the Philippines.

- Financial Inclusion Initiatives: Some play-to-earn projects actively engage in financial inclusion initiatives, such as providing access to banking services or facilitating the transition from virtual to real-world assets. Examining these initiatives provides insights into the role of play-to-earn in promoting financial inclusion.

Community Outreach and Social Impact

- Philanthropy and Community Support: Recognizing the social impact of play-to-earn, some Filipino players and gaming organizations engage in philanthropic activities and community support. This section explores how play-to-earn communities contribute to social causes, providing support to those in need and fostering a sense of responsibility.

- Challenges and Opportunities for Social Impact: While play-to-earn gaming communities have the potential for positive social impact, they also face challenges. Analyzing the dynamics of social impact initiatives sheds light on the opportunities and obstacles faced by these communities in their pursuit of making a difference.

Conclusion: Shaping the Future of Socio-Economic Dynamics

In conclusion, the socio-economic influence of play-to-earn gaming in developing countries like the Philippines is a dynamic and evolving phenomenon. The impact extends from economic empowerment to cultural shifts, educational benefits, and community development. Understanding these dynamics provides valuable insights into the role of play-to-earn in shaping the future of socio-economic dynamics in developing nations.

Issues like Addiction, Unethical Play, and Educational Neglect

Within the realms of play-to-earn gaming, the allure of virtual economies and the pursuit of in-game rewards bring to the forefront a range of complex issues with real-world implications. This chapter delves into the multifaceted challenges of addiction, unethical play, and educational neglect that arise in the context of play-to-earn gaming, exploring their impact on individuals, communities, and the broader socio-cultural landscape.

Understanding Addiction in Play-to-Earn Gaming

- Defining Gaming Addiction: Gaming addiction, often referred to as "gaming disorder," is a recognized mental health condition characterized by excessive and compulsive engagement with video games. This section explores the definition and criteria for gaming addiction, shedding light on how it manifests in the context of play-to-earn gaming.

- Psychological Drivers of Addiction: Examining the psychological drivers behind gaming addiction provides insights into the motivations and behaviors that contribute to excessive gameplay. Understanding the role of rewards, escapism, and social dynamics helps contextualize the challenges associated with addiction in play-to-earn gaming.

- Impact on Mental Health: Addiction to play-to-earn gaming can have profound effects on mental health. This section explores the psychological toll of excessive gameplay, including stress, anxiety, depression, and the potential exacerbation of pre-existing mental health conditions.

Unethical Play Practices and Exploitative Behaviors

- Exploring Unethical Play Practices: Unethical play practices encompass a range of behaviors that violate fair play, exploit loopholes, or engage in activities detrimental to the gaming community. This section delves into the various forms of unethical play, from cheating and exploiting game mechanics to engaging in fraudulent activities within virtual economies.

- Impact on Fairness and Integrity: Unethical play practices compromise the fairness and integrity of play-to-earn ecosystems. Examining their impact on the gaming experience, community trust, and the overall health of virtual economies provides insights into the challenges posed by exploitative behaviors.

- Addressing Exploitative Behaviors: The gaming industry and communities actively seek ways to address and mitigate unethical play practices. This section explores the measures taken to detect and prevent cheating, fraud, and other exploitative behaviors, emphasizing the importance of maintaining a level playing field.

Educational Neglect and its Ramifications

- Neglecting Educational Priorities: As play-to-earn gaming gains prominence, concerns about educational neglect among players emerge. This section explores how excessive gameplay may lead to neglecting educational priorities, impacting academic performance, and potentially hindering personal and professional development.

- Balancing Gaming and Education: Examining strategies for balancing gaming activities with educational responsibilities provides insights into fostering a healthy equilibrium. This involves understanding the role of parental guidance, educational institutions, and self-regulation in promoting a balanced approach to gaming and learning.

- The Role of Gaming in Education: Despite concerns about neglect, play-to-earn gaming also presents opportunities for educational enrichment. This section explores the potential benefits of integrating gaming into educational frameworks, leveraging gamified learning experiences, and encouraging the development of valuable skills through gameplay.

Psychosocial Impact on Relationships and Communities

- Impact on Interpersonal Relationships: Addiction, unethical play, and educational neglect can strain interpersonal relationships, both within families and gaming communities. This section explores the psychosocial impact on relationships, including conflicts, communication breakdowns, and the need for supportive interventions.

- Community Responses to Issues: Gaming communities play a crucial role in addressing and mitigating the psychosocial impact of addiction and unethical play. Examining community-led initiatives, support networks, and awareness campaigns sheds light on the resilience and capacity of gaming communities to respond to these challenges.

- Building Responsible Gaming Communities: Strategies for building responsible gaming communities involve promoting healthy communication, fostering empathy, and implementing community guidelines. This section explores how communities can contribute to creating an environment that prioritizes well-being and ethical play.

Potential Regulatory Measures and Industry Responsibility

- Regulatory Approaches to Addiction: Governments and regulatory bodies are increasingly recognizing the need for measures to address gaming addiction. This section explores potential regulatory approaches, including age restrictions, warning labels, and educational campaigns, aimed at mitigating the risks of addiction.

- Industry Responsibility and Self-regulation: The gaming industry plays a pivotal role in shaping responsible gaming practices. Examining industry-led initiatives, self-regulation efforts, and the development of tools for player well-being highlights the responsibility of game developers and platforms in fostering a healthy gaming environment.

- Balancing Innovation and Player Safety: Striking a balance between fostering innovation in play-to-earn gaming and ensuring player safety is a key consideration. This section explores the challenges and opportunities in aligning industry innovation with ethical and responsible gaming practices.

Support Mechanisms and Mental Health Interventions

- Creating Supportive Environments: Establishing supportive environments involves a collective effort from gaming communities, industry stakeholders, and mental health professionals. This section explores how communities and platforms can create spaces that prioritize well-being, offering support for those affected by addiction, unethical play, or educational neglect.

- Mental Health Interventions: Recognizing the intersection of gaming and mental health, mental health interventions become crucial. This section explores therapeutic approaches, counseling services, and the role of mental health professionals in addressing the challenges posed by addiction and psychosocial impact within gaming communities.

Conclusion: Navigating the Complex Landscape of Challenges

In conclusion, the issues of addiction, unethical play, and educational neglect within play-to-earn gaming form a complex landscape that requires multifaceted responses. Understanding the psychological, social, and regulatory dimensions of these challenges is essential for fostering a gaming environment that prioritizes player well-being, ethical conduct, and a balanced approach to the intersection of virtual and real-world experiences.

Regulatory Responses from Various Global Jurisdictions

The growing prominence of play-to-earn gaming and the associated virtual economies has prompted regulatory scrutiny from jurisdictions worldwide. This chapter delves into the diverse regulatory responses from different global jurisdictions, exploring the approaches taken by governments and regulatory bodies to address the complex challenges and opportunities presented by the evolving landscape of play-to-earn gaming.

Understanding the Regulatory Landscape

- Defining Regulatory Frameworks: The regulatory landscape for play-to-earn gaming is multifaceted, encompassing aspects of gaming, finance, and technology. This section provides an overview of the regulatory frameworks that influence play-to-earn ecosystems, considering the intersection of gaming regulations, financial laws, and emerging technologies.

- Jurisdictional Variances: Different countries exhibit varied approaches to regulating play-to-earn gaming, reflecting unique legal, cultural, and economic considerations. Examining jurisdictional variances sheds light on the complexities of creating a cohesive regulatory framework for a global and decentralized industry.

Challenges and Concerns Addressed by Regulations

- Player Protection and Rights: Regulatory responses often prioritize player protection and rights. This section explores how regulations aim to ensure fair play, prevent fraud, and safeguard the rights of players within virtual economies, addressing concerns related to in-game assets, digital property, and contractual agreements.

- Financial Integrity and Anti-Fraud Measures: Financial integrity is a paramount concern in play-to-earn gaming. Regulatory responses include anti-fraud measures, Know Your Customer (KYC) requirements, and mechanisms to combat money laundering within virtual economies. Analyzing these measures provides insights into efforts to maintain financial transparency.

- Consumer Education and Awareness: Some regulatory approaches emphasize consumer education and awareness, aiming to inform players about the risks, rewards, and responsible practices within play-to-earn ecosystems. Examining these educational initiatives highlights the role of regulations in promoting informed and empowered player communities.

Diverse Approaches to Virtual Assets and Cryptocurrencies

- Legal Status of Virtual Assets: The legal status of virtual assets, including in-game items and cryptocurrencies, varies globally. This section explores how different jurisdictions classify and regulate virtual assets, addressing questions of ownership, taxation, and the legal recognition of digital property.

- Cryptocurrency Regulations: Play-to-earn ecosystems often involve the use of cryptocurrencies for in-game transactions. Regulatory responses to cryptocurrency usage vary, with some countries embracing innovative financial technologies and others implementing stringent regulations. Analyzing these responses provides insights into the evolving regulatory landscape for blockchain-based transactions.

Emergence of Decentralized Finance (DeFi) Regulations

- Integration of DeFi Protocols: Play-to-earn ecosystems increasingly integrate decentralized finance (DeFi) protocols, introducing new regulatory considerations. This section explores how regulators grapple with the complexities of decentralized financial services within virtual gaming economies, including issues of governance, transparency, and risk management.

- Smart Contract Audits and Security: Regulatory responses may address the security aspects of smart contracts and DeFi protocols within play-to-earn gaming. Examining how regulators approach smart contract audits, vulnerability disclosures, and security best practices provides insights into efforts to mitigate risks associated with blockchain-based financial services.

Global Collaboration and Standardization Efforts

- International Collaboration: Some regulatory responses involve international collaboration and coordination to address the global nature of play-to-earn gaming. This section explores initiatives, partnerships, and dialogues between regulatory bodies to create standardized approaches and best practices for regulating virtual economies.

- Industry Self-Regulation: The play-to-earn gaming industry is actively engaged in self-regulation efforts. This involves the development of industry standards, codes of conduct, and self-regulatory bodies to proactively address regulatory concerns and foster a cooperative relationship with authorities.

Impact of Regulations on Innovation and Industry Growth

- Balancing Innovation and Regulation: Striking a balance between fostering innovation and implementing effective regulations is a central challenge. This section examines how regulatory responses aim to support innovation within play-to-earn gaming while ensuring consumer protection, financial integrity, and adherence to legal standards.

- Encouraging Responsible Development: Regulatory frameworks can influence the responsible development of play-to-earn ecosystems. This involves creating an environment where developers, entrepreneurs, and investors can contribute to the industry's growth while adhering to ethical and legal standards.

Case Studies: Regulatory Approaches in Key Jurisdictions

- United States: Explore how regulatory bodies in the United States, such as the Securities and Exchange Commission (SEC) and the Commodity Futures Trading Commission (CFTC), approach the regulation of play-to-earn gaming, considering legal precedents, enforcement actions, and evolving policy perspectives.

- European Union: Examine the regulatory landscape in the European Union, including initiatives by the European Securities and Markets Authority (ESMA) and individual member states. This section delves into the challenges of harmonizing regulations across diverse national jurisdictions.

- Southeast Asia: Investigate the regulatory responses from countries in Southeast Asia, a region witnessing significant growth in play-to-earn gaming. Case studies may include approaches taken by regulatory bodies in Singapore, the Philippines, and Malaysia.

- China: Analyze China's regulatory stance on play-to-earn gaming, considering the role of governmental bodies like the State Administration of Press and Publication (SAPP) and their impact on the gaming industry.

The Role of Regulations in Shaping the Industry's Future

- Evolving Regulatory Landscapes: Regulatory responses to play-to-earn gaming are dynamic and evolving. This section examines how regulatory landscapes adapt to technological advancements, industry innovations, and changing player behaviors, providing insights into the ongoing evolution of regulations.

- Anticipating Future Challenges: Anticipating future challenges involves considering the potential impacts of emerging technologies, market trends, and player behaviors. This section explores how regulatory bodies proactively address challenges, foster industry resilience, and prepare for the continued growth of play-to-earn gaming.

Conclusion: Navigating a Complex Regulatory Terrain

In conclusion, the regulatory responses from various global jurisdictions play a pivotal role in shaping the trajectory of play-to-earn gaming. Navigating this complex terrain involves addressing diverse concerns, fostering innovation, and striking a delicate balance between player empowerment and regulatory oversight. Understanding the nuances of these regulatory responses provides valuable insights into the industry's maturation and its integration into the broader regulatory frameworks of the global economy.

Mainstream Perceptions and Media Narratives

The real-world impacts of play-to-earn gaming extend beyond the virtual realm and into the consciousness of mainstream society. This chapter explores how play-to-earn gaming is perceived by the general public, dissecting media narratives, and shedding light on the factors that shape the broader societal understanding of this burgeoning phenomenon.

Perceptions of Play-to-Earn Gaming in Mainstream Culture

- Defining Play-to-Earn for Mainstream Audiences: Introducing play-to-earn gaming to a mainstream audience requires a clear definition. This section explores the challenges of articulating the concept to individuals unfamiliar with the gaming landscape, establishing a foundation for understanding within broader cultural contexts.

- Navigating Misconceptions: Play-to-earn gaming often faces misconceptions, from being labeled as mere entertainment to concerns about its impact on productivity. This section addresses common misconceptions and clarifies the distinctions between play-to-earn gaming and traditional gaming models.

Media Representations and Storytelling

- Portrayal in News Outlets: Analyzing how play-to-earn gaming is portrayed in traditional news outlets provides insights into the framing of stories, the language used, and the overall tone of media coverage. Examining news articles, features, and interviews helps uncover patterns in how the industry is presented to the public.

- Documentary Narratives: Documentaries have become a powerful medium for exploring complex topics. This section delves into the narratives presented in documentaries about play-to-earn gaming, considering how filmmakers choose to tell the story, the perspectives they highlight, and the impact on audience perceptions.

- Influence of Feature Articles and Op-Eds: Feature articles and opinion pieces play a significant role in shaping public opinion. Exploring influential pieces within mainstream media provides insights into the narratives that gain prominence, the voices shaping the discourse, and the potential biases that may emerge.

Cultural Commentary and Editorial Perspectives

- Cultural Context and Commentary: Play-to-earn gaming exists within a broader cultural context. This section examines cultural commentary on play-to-earn, exploring how societal values, norms, and trends influence the way the phenomenon is discussed and understood in mainstream discourse.

- Editorial Perspectives on Economic Impacts: Economic implications of play-to-earn gaming are often a focal point of media coverage. This section analyzes editorials and economic commentaries, exploring how mainstream media assesses the economic significance, opportunities, and challenges posed by play-to-earn models.

Representation of Players and Gaming Communities

- Player Profiles and Human Stories: Humanizing the experience of play-to-earn participants through player profiles and personal narratives helps bridge the gap between the virtual and real worlds. This section explores how mainstream media represents the stories of individual players, their motivations, and the impact of play-to-earn on their lives.

- Community Features and Spotlights: Gaming communities within play-to-earn ecosystems contribute to the broader narrative. Examining community features and spotlights in mainstream media provides insights into how these communities are portrayed, the diversity of player experiences, and the societal dynamics they embody.

Challenges and Controversies in Media Coverage

- Addressing Controversies: Media coverage of play-to-earn gaming is not without its controversies. This section explores instances of negative publicity, controversies, and ethical debates within mainstream media, considering how these challenges impact public perception and the industry's reputation.

- Balancing Positive and Negative Narratives: Achieving a balanced portrayal of play-to-earn gaming involves navigating both positive and negative narratives. This section assesses how media outlets strike a balance, considering the role of journalistic responsibility and the potential consequences of skewed representations.

Influence of Celebrity Endorsements and Pop Culture

- Celebrity Perspectives and Endorsements: Celebrity endorsements can significantly impact public perceptions. This section explores how celebrities, influencers, and public figures contribute to the narrative around play-to-earn gaming, considering their influence on mainstream culture and public opinion.

- Integration into Pop Culture: Play-to-earn gaming's integration into pop culture is a key indicator of its societal impact. This section examines how the phenomenon is depicted in popular culture, including references in music, movies, television, and other forms of entertainment.

Comparative Analysis of Global Perspectives

- Regional Variances in Media Coverage: Media coverage of play-to-earn gaming varies across regions. This section conducts a comparative analysis, exploring how different countries and cultures frame the narrative, examining regional nuances, and considering the impact of cultural differences on mainstream perceptions.

- Public Opinion Polls and Surveys: Quantifying public opinion through polls and surveys provides additional context to media narratives. This section explores the results of public opinion studies, considering the factors that influence attitudes toward play-to-earn gaming and how these findings align with or challenge media representations.

Media's Role in Shaping Public Opinion and Understanding

- Media as a Shaper of Perceptions: The media plays a crucial role in shaping public opinion. This section explores the influence of media narratives on the formation of attitudes and beliefs about play-to-earn gaming, considering how these narratives contribute to the broader societal understanding of the phenomenon.

- Responsibility of Media Outlets: Assessing the responsibility of media outlets involves considering ethical considerations, journalistic standards, and the potential impact of media narratives on public perception. This section examines the role of media in responsibly covering play-to-earn gaming and fostering a nuanced understanding among audiences.

Conclusion: Navigating the Media Landscape of Play-to-Earn Gaming

In conclusion, the mainstream perceptions and media narratives surrounding play-to-earn gaming are dynamic and multifaceted. Navigating this media landscape involves understanding the nuances of representation, analyzing the factors influencing public opinion, and considering the role of media outlets in shaping the broader societal understanding of this evolving phenomenon. As play-to-earn gaming continues to capture public attention, the media's role in conveying its complexities and impact remains a critical aspect of the industry's integration into mainstream culture.

Grassroots Player Stories and Testimonials

At the heart of play-to-earn gaming are the individual stories and testimonials of players who have experienced firsthand the transformative impact of these virtual economies on their lives. This chapter delves into the grassroots level, exploring the diverse narratives of players from different backgrounds, regions, and walks of life, shedding light on the personal journeys, challenges, and successes within the play-to-earn gaming ecosystem.

Capturing the Essence of Player Experiences

- Diversity of Player Profiles: The world of play-to-earn gaming attracts a diverse array of players, each with a unique story to tell. This section introduces readers to the rich tapestry of player profiles, spanning various demographics, professions, and interests. By exploring these diverse backgrounds, the chapter sets the stage for understanding the broad spectrum of experiences within play-to-earn communities.

- Motivations for Participation: Understanding why players choose to participate in play-to-earn gaming is crucial. This section explores the motivations that drive individuals to enter these virtual economies, whether driven by economic incentives, a passion for gaming, or a desire for community engagement. By examining the diverse motivations, the chapter paints a nuanced picture of player engagement.

From Novice to Expert: Evolution of Player Journeys

- Early Experiences and Learning Curves: Many players begin their play-to-earn journey as novices, navigating the complexities of blockchain technology, in-game economies, and community dynamics. This section shares stories of early experiences and the learning curves players face, providing insights into the initial challenges and triumphs of those new to the play-to-earn ecosystem.

- Skill Development and Mastery: As players progress within play-to-earn games, they often develop and hone skills that extend beyond traditional gaming. This section explores the stories of players who have achieved mastery in various aspects of play-to-earn, whether through strategic gameplay, market analysis, or community leadership. These narratives highlight the multifaceted nature of skill development within virtual economies.

Community Connections and Collaborations

- Formation of Player Communities: Play-to-earn gaming is not just about individual players but also about the communities they form. This section explores the narratives of players coming together to create and sustain communities, whether through guilds, alliances, or collaborative projects. By examining these stories, the chapter provides a glimpse into the social fabric of play-to-earn ecosystems.

- Collaborative Ventures and Achievements: Beyond individual achievements, players often collaborate on ventures that impact the broader play-to-earn community. This section shares stories of collaborative projects, in-game events, and community-driven initiatives that contribute to the overall growth and vibrancy of play-to-earn gaming.

Overcoming Challenges and Adversities

- Financial Impact on Real Lives: Play-to-earn gaming has the potential to make a tangible difference in the lives of players. This section features stories of individuals whose financial situations have been positively impacted by their involvement in play-to-earn ecosystems. By exploring these narratives, the chapter examines the real-world economic implications of virtual economies.

- Navigating Setbacks and Losses: Not every player journey is without challenges. This section shares stories of players who have faced setbacks, losses, or unexpected challenges within play-to-earn gaming. By highlighting these narratives, the chapter explores the resilience and adaptability of players in the face of adversity.

Passion, Creativity, and Player-Generated Content

- Passionate Pursuits: Many players are drawn to play-to-earn gaming not just for financial gain but also for the sheer passion and enjoyment it brings. This section explores stories of players who pursue play-to-earn activities out of love for the game, creativity, or a desire to contribute meaningfully to the virtual worlds they inhabit.

- Player-Generated Content and Artistry: Play-to-earn communities often foster creativity and artistic expression. This section showcases stories of players who contribute to the richness of virtual worlds through player-generated content, fan art, storytelling, and other creative endeavors. These narratives highlight the symbiotic relationship between players and the virtual universes they inhabit.

Impact on Well-Being and Lifestyle

- Balancing Play and Real Life: Achieving a balance between play-to-earn activities and real-life responsibilities is a common challenge for players. This section explores stories of individuals who have successfully navigated this balance, sharing insights into effective time management, priorities, and the integration of play-to-earn into daily life.

- Positive Well-Being Outcomes: Engaging in play-to-earn gaming can have positive effects on players' well-being. This section features narratives of individuals who attribute improved mental health, a sense of purpose, or enhanced social connections to their experiences within play-to-earn ecosystems. By examining these stories, the chapter explores the holistic impact of virtual economies on player well-being.

Testimonials of Transformation and Personal Growth

- Stories of Transformation: Some players undergo profound personal transformations as a result of their play-to-earn experiences. This section shares stories of individuals who have experienced significant life changes, whether in career paths, personal goals, or self-discovery, through their participation in play-to-earn gaming.

- Reflections on Personal Growth: Players often reflect on the growth and development they've experienced within play-to-earn ecosystems. This section features testimonials that delve into the self-discovery, skill acquisition, and personal growth that players attribute to their engagement with virtual economies.

Voices of the Player Community: Testimonials and Reflections

- Compiling Player Testimonials: This section compiles direct testimonials from players, allowing them to share their experiences, insights, and reflections in their own words. By presenting authentic voices from the play-to-earn community, the chapter provides readers with a direct and unfiltered connection to the diverse narratives within the ecosystem.

Conclusion: Celebrating the Human Stories of Play-to-Earn Gaming

In conclusion, the grassroots player stories and testimonials presented in this chapter offer a window into the diverse and dynamic world of play-to-earn gaming. By celebrating the individual journeys, achievements, challenges, and personal growth of players, the chapter highlights the human dimension of virtual economies and emphasizes the profound impact that play-to-earn experiences can have on real lives.

Chapter 8 - Institutional Investment and Adoption Crypto Funds Investing Hundreds of Millions in Play-to-Earn Networks

In the evolving landscape of play-to-earn gaming, institutional investors and crypto funds have recognized the potential of virtual economies and blockchain-based gaming platforms. This chapter explores the substantial investments made by crypto funds into play-to-earn networks, delving into the motivations behind these investments, the impact on the gaming industry, and the broader implications for the future of virtual economies.

The Rise of Institutional Interest in Play-to-Earn

- Recognition of Gaming as an Emerging Asset Class: Institutional investors have started to view play-to-earn gaming as more than just entertainment; it's now considered an emerging asset class with unique economic opportunities. This section examines the factors that led to the recognition of gaming as a viable investment, including the growth of virtual economies, player engagement metrics, and the integration of blockchain technology.

- Understanding the Appeal of Virtual Economies: Virtual economies within play-to-earn games present new investment possibilities. This section explores the appeal of these economies to institutional investors, including the potential for revenue generation, the novel tokenomic structures, and the decentralized nature of blockchain-based gaming platforms.

Major Crypto Funds and Their Investments

- Overview of Leading Crypto Funds: This section provides an overview of prominent crypto funds that have actively invested in play-to-earn networks. Names like Andreessen Horowitz, Pantera Capital, and Galaxy Digital have entered the space, signaling a significant shift in the perception of gaming within the broader crypto investment landscape.

- Case Studies of Significant Investments: Highlighting specific case studies, this part of the chapter delves into major investments made by crypto funds in play-to-earn networks. Examining the funding rounds, valuation trends, and strategic partnerships, readers gain insights into the financial dynamics that drive these investments.

Motivations Behind Crypto Funds' Investments

- Diversification and Portfolio Expansion: Institutional investors seek to diversify their portfolios to manage risk and capture emerging opportunities. This section explores how play-to-earn investments contribute to the diversification goals of crypto funds, providing exposure to a rapidly growing sector outside traditional asset classes.

- Long-Term Growth Potential: Crypto funds often adopt a long-term investment perspective. This part of the chapter analyzes how play-to-earn gaming aligns with the long-term growth expectations of institutional investors, considering factors such as user adoption, technological advancements, and the evolving dynamics of virtual economies.

- Alignment with Decentralization Principles: Institutional investors attracted to blockchain technology often prioritize projects that align with decentralization principles. This section examines how play-to-earn networks, built on blockchain infrastructure, resonate with the decentralized ethos, attracting funds seeking projects with robust and transparent governance structures.

Impact on Play-to-Earn Platforms and Game Studios

- Acceleration of Development and Innovation: The influx of significant funding accelerates the development and innovation within play-to-earn platforms and game studios.

This section explores how substantial investments enable these entities to enhance their technological capabilities, expand their gaming ecosystems, and pioneer new features that contribute to the overall advancement of the play-to-earn space.

- Strategic Collaborations and Partnerships: Investments from crypto funds often lead to strategic collaborations between play-to-earn platforms and established blockchain projects. This part of the chapter investigates how such collaborations strengthen the infrastructure, interoperability, and utility of play-to-earn networks, fostering a more interconnected and robust ecosystem.

Challenges and Considerations for Institutional Investors

- Volatility and Market Risks: Institutional investors face unique challenges in the volatile and dynamic crypto market. This section discusses how the inherent volatility of cryptocurrencies and the nascent nature of play-to-earn ecosystems pose risks that investors must navigate strategically.

- Regulatory Landscape: The regulatory environment plays a crucial role in shaping institutional investments. This part of the chapter examines how the evolving regulatory landscape impacts the decisions of crypto funds, considering compliance, legal considerations, and the potential influence of regulatory developments on play-to-earn investments.

Market Impact and Growth Trajectory

- Market Valuation and Trends: The investments from crypto funds influence the market valuation and trends within the play-to-earn space. This section explores how significant funding rounds contribute to the overall valuation of play-to-earn platforms and the subsequent market trends that emerge as a result.

- Projection of Future Investment Trends: Looking ahead, this part of the chapter provides insights into the projected trends of institutional investments in play-to-earn gaming. Factors such as emerging technologies, user adoption metrics, and market maturity are considered to forecast the trajectory of future investment flows.

Broader Implications for the Gaming Industry

- Legitimizing Gaming as an Investment Sector: The substantial investments from crypto funds contribute to legitimizing gaming as a viable investment sector. This section discusses how this legitimacy enhances the overall perception of play-to-earn gaming within the broader financial and gaming industries.

- Influence on Traditional Game Studios: The impact of institutional investments in play-to-earn extends beyond blockchain-native platforms. This part of the chapter explores how traditional game studios respond to the growing interest from crypto funds, considering potential collaborations, adoption of blockchain technology, and the convergence of traditional and blockchain-based gaming models.

Conclusion: Shaping the Future of Virtual Economies

In conclusion, the involvement of crypto funds and institutional investors in play-to-earn gaming marks a pivotal moment in the evolution of virtual economies. The substantial investments bring not only financial support but also validation and strategic partnerships that propel the growth and innovation of play-to-earn platforms. As institutional interest continues to shape the landscape, the future holds the promise of a more interconnected, sophisticated, and widely adopted play-to-earn ecosystem, redefining the intersection of gaming, blockchain technology, and institutional finance.

Large Game Studios like Ubisoft and Atari Entering the Play-to-Earn Market

In recent years, the landscape of play-to-earn gaming has witnessed a transformative shift with the entry of established gaming giants like Ubisoft and Atari. This chapter explores the motivations behind these major game studios entering the play-to-earn market, their impact on the industry, and the implications for the future of virtual economies.

The Paradigm Shift: Traditional Game Studios Embracing Play-to-Earn

- Evolution of Gaming Business Models: Traditional game studios, long accustomed to traditional revenue models, have recognized the potential of play-to-earn gaming. This section explores the paradigm shift in the industry, analyzing how large studios are adapting to the changing landscape and integrating play-to-earn elements into their game design and monetization strategies.

- Strategic Vision for Blockchain Integration: Understanding the strategic vision behind large game studios entering the play-to-earn space is crucial. This part of the chapter delves into how studios like Ubisoft and Atari perceive the value of blockchain technology, decentralized economies, and player-owned assets, shaping their decisions to explore play-to-earn models.

Ubisoft: Navigating the Play-to-Earn Frontier

- Overview of Ubisoft's Entry: Ubisoft, a prominent name in the gaming industry, has stepped into the play-to-earn arena. This section provides an in-depth look at Ubisoft's foray into play-to-earn, examining specific projects, partnerships, and initiatives that showcase the studio's commitment to exploring the potential of blockchain-based gaming.

- Integration of Play-to-Earn in Existing Titles: Ubisoft's entry into play-to-earn involves integrating these elements into existing titles. This part of the chapter explores how established franchises are adapting to the play-to-earn model, the challenges faced, and the reception from the gaming community.

- Strategic Partnerships and Collaborations: Large game studios often forge strategic partnerships to strengthen their presence in the play-to-earn space. This section analyzes Ubisoft's collaborations within the blockchain and crypto space, exploring the synergies that emerge from alliances with blockchain projects, platforms, and communities.

Atari: Pioneering Play-to-Earn in Gaming History

- Atari's Relevance in Modern Gaming: Atari, an iconic name synonymous with the early days of gaming, has reemerged with a focus on blockchain and play-to-earn. This part of the chapter provides an overview of Atari's historical significance, its resurgence, and the strategic decisions that led to its exploration of play-to-earn gaming.

- Atari's Play-to-Earn Initiatives: Atari's play-to-earn initiatives go beyond conventional gaming approaches. This section explores specific projects and ventures undertaken by Atari in the play-to-earn space, shedding light on the studio's unique contributions to the evolution of virtual economies.

- Innovation and NFT Integration: Atari's approach to play-to-earn involves innovative use of non-fungible tokens (NFTs) and blockchain technology. This part of the chapter examines how Atari is integrating NFTs into its gaming ecosystem, exploring the implications for ownership, scarcity, and player engagement.

Motivations and Strategies of Large Game Studios

- Diversification and Market Expansion: The motivations of large game studios to enter the play-to-earn market extend beyond experimentation. This section explores how diversification and expansion into blockchain-based gaming align with the strategic goals of studios like Ubisoft and Atari, offering insights into their broader market positioning.

- Addressing Evolving Player Expectations: Large game studios recognize the evolving expectations of players in an era of decentralized economies. This part of the chapter examines how the play-to-earn model caters to changing player preferences, fostering engagement, and creating new avenues for interaction within gaming communities.

- Unlocking New Revenue Streams: Traditional revenue streams in gaming are supplemented by new opportunities presented by play-to-earn. This section explores how large game studios view play-to-earn as a means to unlock additional revenue streams, diversifying their financial models and ensuring sustainability in a dynamic industry.

Impact on Gaming Ecosystems and Player Communities

- Engaging Established Player Bases: Large game studios entering the play-to-earn market have access to substantial player bases. This part of the chapter explores how these studios leverage their existing audiences, introducing play-to-earn elements to engage established player communities and bridge the gap between traditional and blockchain-based gaming.

- Influence on Game Design and Development: The entry of major studios introduces new dynamics to game design and development. This section examines how play-to-earn considerations impact the creative process, from conceptualization to execution, and the evolving role of player feedback in shaping the direction of these projects.

Challenges and Considerations for Large Game Studios

- Navigating Regulatory Complexity: The regulatory landscape surrounding blockchain and play-to-earn gaming poses challenges for large studios. This section delves into the considerations and strategies employed by studios like Ubisoft and Atari to navigate regulatory complexities, ensuring compliance and legal adherence.

- Balancing Traditional and Blockchain Gaming Models: Large game studios face the task of balancing traditional gaming models with the innovative elements of blockchain-based play-to-earn. This part of the chapter explores the challenges and approaches these studios adopt to maintain equilibrium between the two models, ensuring a seamless experience for players.

Future Trajectory and Industry Collaboration

- Predicting the Future of Large Studios in Play-to-Earn: What lies ahead for large game studios in the play-to-earn space? This section provides insights into the potential trajectory of Ubisoft, Atari, and other major players in the evolving landscape, considering industry trends, technological advancements, and player expectations.

- Collaboration and Cross-Industry Influence: Large game studios entering play-to-earn bring with them the potential for cross-industry collaborations. This part of the chapter explores how collaborations between traditional gaming, blockchain technology, and play-to-earn initiatives can shape the future of the broader gaming ecosystem.

Conclusion: The Convergence of Tradition and Innovation

In conclusion, the entry of large game studios like Ubisoft and Atari into the play-to-earn market signifies a convergence of tradition and innovation within the gaming industry. As these studios navigate the complexities of blockchain technology and decentralized economies, they contribute to the ongoing transformation of virtual economies, player expectations, and the very essence of gaming. The implications of their involvement extend beyond individual projects, shaping the future of play-to-earn on a broader scale, and marking a pivotal moment in the evolution of the gaming industry.

Partnerships with Global Brands like Adidas, Samsung, and Others: The Symbiosis of Play-to-Earn and Corporate Giants

The fusion of play-to-earn gaming with global brands such as Adidas, Samsung, and others represents a strategic alliance that extends beyond the gaming realm. This chapter explores the motivations, impact, and implications of partnerships between play-to-earn platforms and iconic global brands, examining the symbiotic relationship that emerges when virtual economies meet corporate giants.

The Rise of Collaborations: Play-to-Earn Meets Corporate Giants

- Shifting Dynamics in Brand Partnerships: Traditional advertising channels are evolving, and brands are increasingly recognizing the potential of play-to-earn platforms as a unique avenue for engagement. This section delves into the changing dynamics of brand partnerships, highlighting the reasons behind global brands venturing into the play-to-earn space.

- Motivations for Global Brands: Global brands such as Adidas and Samsung are drawn to play-to-earn partnerships for various reasons. This part of the chapter explores the motivations behind these collaborations, including reaching new audiences, innovative marketing strategies, and the alignment of brand values with the principles of decentralized economies.

Case Studies: Iconic Collaborations in Play-to-Earn Gaming

- Adidas: Stepping into the Virtual Arena: Adidas, a global leader in the sportswear industry, has entered the play-to-earn arena. This section provides an in-depth exploration of Adidas's foray into the virtual space, examining specific projects, campaigns, and initiatives that exemplify the brand's engagement with play-to-earn gaming.

- Samsung: Bridging the Gap Between Real and Virtual: Samsung, a tech giant, has embraced the virtual realm through collaborations with play-to-earn platforms. This part of the chapter investigates Samsung's entry into play-to-earn, analyzing key projects, technological integrations, and the brand's strategy to bridge the gap between the physical and virtual worlds.

- Other Notable Collaborations: Beyond Adidas and Samsung, numerous other global brands have ventured into play-to-earn partnerships. This section provides an overview of diverse collaborations, exploring how brands from various industries contribute to the enrichment of virtual economies and the gaming experience.

Mutual Benefits of Play-to-Earn and Brand Collaborations

- Expanding Audience Reach: Collaborations with global brands extend the reach of play-to-earn platforms to new demographics. This section examines how partnerships introduce play-to-earn gaming to audiences beyond traditional gamers, fostering a more inclusive and diverse community.

- Innovative Marketing and Brand Exposure: The marriage of play-to-earn and global brands opens avenues for innovative marketing strategies. This part of the chapter explores how these collaborations provide unique opportunities for brand exposure, creative campaigns, and the integration of virtual items into real-world marketing initiatives.

- Enhancing User Engagement and Retention: The symbiotic relationship between play-to-earn and global brands contributes to enhanced user engagement and retention. This section delves into how branded collaborations introduce new dynamics to gameplay, offer exclusive rewards, and create memorable experiences that keep players invested in the virtual worlds.

Challenges and Considerations in Brand-Play-to-Earn Collaborations

- Maintaining Brand Authenticity: As global brands enter the play-to-earn space, maintaining authenticity becomes crucial. This section explores the challenges brands face in aligning their virtual presence with their real-world identity, ensuring that the essence of the brand is preserved within the gaming context.

- Navigating Regulatory and Ethical Considerations: Collaborations between play-to-earn platforms and global brands raise regulatory and ethical considerations. This part of the chapter examines how these partnerships navigate legal frameworks, ethical guidelines, and potential controversies that may arise in the intersection of virtual economies and corporate branding.

Impact on Virtual Economies and In-Game Experiences

- Integration of Branded Virtual Items: The integration of branded virtual items within play-to-earn games is a notable outcome of these collaborations. This section explores how iconic brands contribute to the in-game experience by introducing exclusive virtual assets, wearables, and customization options.

- Economic Implications of Branded Partnerships: Branded collaborations influence the economic dynamics of virtual economies. This part of the chapter investigates how the introduction of branded items affects in-game economies, player trading behavior, and the overall valuation of virtual assets.

Future Trajectory of Brand-Play-to-Earn Collaborations

- Evolution of Partnerships: The future holds the promise of continued evolution in brand-play-to-earn collaborations. This section provides insights into how partnerships with global brands may evolve, considering emerging technologies, changing consumer behaviors, and the dynamic nature of both the gaming and branding industries.

- Potential for Cross-Industry Collaborations: Beyond individual collaborations, the chapter explores the potential for cross-industry partnerships between play-to-earn platforms and brands from diverse sectors. How collaborations may extend to areas such as fashion, technology, entertainment, and more is considered, offering a glimpse into the interconnected future of virtual economies.

Conclusion: Shaping the Convergence of Virtual and Corporate Realities

In conclusion, the partnerships between play-to-earn platforms and global brands mark a convergence of virtual and corporate realities. As iconic brands step into the virtual arena, they not only contribute to the growth of play-to-earn gaming but also redefine the landscape of digital marketing and brand engagement. The implications extend beyond the virtual realms, shaping the way audiences interact with both virtual economies and real-world brands, and opening new frontiers for innovation and collaboration in the ever-evolving landscape of play-to-earn gaming.

Mass Media and Entertainment's Fascination: Play-to-Earn in Movies, Documentaries, and Beyond

The allure of play-to-earn gaming has transcended the virtual realm, capturing the attention of mass media and the entertainment industry. This chapter explores the intersection of play-to-earn with movies, documentaries, and other forms of mass media, shedding light on the symbiotic relationship between virtual economies and the storytelling prowess of the entertainment world.

The Cinematic Journey: Play-to-Earn on the Silver Screen

- Play-to-Earn as a Narrative Device: Filmmakers have recognized the narrative potential embedded in play-to-earn gaming. This section delves into how play-to-earn serves as more than just a backdrop, becoming a central element of storytelling in movies. From plot devices to character motivations, the integration of virtual economies adds a layer of complexity to cinematic narratives.

- Exploration of Virtual Worlds: Movies exploring the vast landscapes of play-to-earn virtual worlds offer audiences a glimpse into the immersive environments that gamers experience. This part of the chapter examines how filmmakers bring these virtual landscapes to life, leveraging cutting-edge visual effects and storytelling techniques to transport viewers into the heart of play-to-earn adventures.

- Character Arcs and Economic Realities: Characters navigating play-to-earn environments undergo unique arcs shaped by the economic dynamics of virtual worlds. This section analyzes how filmmakers depict character growth, challenges, and triumphs within the context of virtual economies, mirroring the experiences of real players.

From Pixels to Projectors: Documentaries Unveiling Play-to-Earn Realities

- Documentary Explorations of Play-to-Earn: Documentaries have emerged as powerful tools to unveil the realities of play-to-earn gaming. This part of the chapter explores how documentaries delve into the history, challenges, and triumphs of play-to-earn, offering audiences an authentic and informative glimpse into the evolution of virtual economies.

- Player Stories and Testimonials: Documentaries often feature the stories of real players, providing a human touch to the virtual narrative. This section investigates how player testimonials become central components of play-to-earn documentaries, illustrating the real-world impact of virtual economies on individuals and communities.

Entertainment Beyond the Screens: Series, Animations, and More

- Serialized Storytelling in TV Series: Play-to-earn has found its way into serialized storytelling, with TV series exploring the intricacies of virtual economies over multiple episodes. This section analyzes how TV series weave play-to-earn elements into ongoing narratives, captivating audiences with long-form storytelling and character development.

- Animated Worlds and Virtual Adventures: Animation becomes a vibrant canvas for the expression of play-to-earn dynamics. This part of the chapter explores how animated content brings playful and fantastical elements of virtual economies to life, catering to diverse audiences and creating memorable characters and worlds.

- Literary Adaptations and Play-to-Earn Novels: The influence of play-to-earn extends into literature, with novels and literary works exploring the themes and narratives inherent in virtual economies. This section examines how authors adapt play-to-earn concepts into compelling narratives, reaching audiences through the power of written storytelling.

Behind the Scenes: The Making of Play-to-Earn Entertainment

- Collaborations Between Filmmakers and Gaming Studios: The chapter explores the collaborations between filmmakers and gaming studios, highlighting how these partnerships shape the cinematic portrayal of play-to-earn. From advisory roles to direct involvement in production, gaming studios contribute their expertise to ensure an authentic representation of virtual economies on the big screen.

- Challenges in Translating Virtual to Visual: Filmmakers encounter unique challenges when translating the visual spectacle of play-to-earn into cinematic experiences. This section examines the hurdles faced by directors, writers, and producers in capturing the essence of virtual economies while catering to a broad audience.

The Impact Beyond Entertainment: Cultural Shifts and Community Reflections

- Cultural Shifts and Mainstream Perceptions: Play-to-earn's portrayal in mass media influences mainstream perceptions. This part of the chapter explores how cinematic and televised representations shape cultural attitudes toward virtual economies, impacting how society views gaming, ownership, and the convergence of virtual and real worlds.

- Community Reflections and Feedback: The depiction of play-to-earn in mass media sparks discussions within gaming communities. This section delves into how player communities react to on-screen representations, exploring the feedback loop between mass media portrayals and the lived experiences of players within virtual economies.

Future Visions: The Evolution of Play-to-Earn in Entertainment

- Anticipating Future Cinematic Explorations: The chapter concludes by speculating on the future of play-to-earn in mass media and entertainment. From upcoming movie releases to evolving documentary formats, this section offers insights into the potential directions in which play-to-earn narratives may unfold in the entertainment landscape.

Conclusion: The Synergy of Stories and Virtual Economies

In conclusion, the intertwining of play-to-earn gaming with mass media and entertainment represents a synergy of stories and virtual economies. From cinematic adventures that bring virtual worlds to life on the silver screen to documentaries that unveil the realities of player experiences, the chapter explores how play-to-earn becomes a compelling narrative thread in the rich tapestry of entertainment. As these stories unfold, they contribute not only to the entertainment industry but also to the broader cultural dialogue surrounding gaming, ownership, and the transformative potential of virtual economies.

Celebrities as Catalysts: Play-to-Earn Thrust into the Spotlight

The fusion of play-to-earn gaming with celebrity endorsements has propelled the decentralized virtual economies into mainstream consciousness. This chapter explores the influential role played by celebrities, such as Snoop Dogg and sports stars, in promoting and endorsing play-to-earn platforms, shedding light on the symbiotic relationship between fame, fortune, and the burgeoning world of virtual economies.

The Celebrity Stamp of Approval: Snoop Dogg and Play-to-Earn

- Snoop Dogg's Entry into the Gaming Arena: This section delves into the foray of Snoop Dogg, the iconic rapper and entrepreneur, into the play-to-earn gaming space. Exploring his gaming interests, collaborations, and virtual endeavors, the chapter highlights how Snoop Dogg became a prominent figure in bridging the gap between celebrity culture and the gaming community.

- Influence Beyond Music: Snoop Dogg's influence extends beyond his music career, encompassing diverse industries. This part of the chapter examines how Snoop Dogg's entry into play-to-earn brings a unique blend of pop culture and gaming, attracting a wider audience and adding a layer of cultural relevance to virtual economies.

- Collaborations and Exclusive Drops: Snoop Dogg's collaborations with play-to-earn platforms often involve exclusive drops and in-game events. This section analyzes the impact of these collaborations on user engagement, platform visibility, and the overall integration of celebrity personas into the fabric of virtual economies.

Sports Stars on the Digital Playground: Athletic Endorsements in Play-to-Earn

- Professional Athletes as Play-to-Earn Advocates: The chapter explores how professional athletes, ranging from football stars to basketball legends, have embraced and advocated for play-to-earn gaming. It investigates their motivations, engagements, and the ways in which their involvement amplifies the convergence of sports and virtual economies.

- From Stadiums to Virtual Arenas: Sports stars bring their competitive spirit from physical arenas to virtual spaces. This part of the chapter examines how athletes navigate play-to-earn platforms, participate in virtual competitions, and engage with fans in the digital realm, creating new dimensions for both sports and gaming enthusiasts.

The Impact of Celebrity Endorsements on Play-to-Earn Platforms

- Boosting User Acquisition and Retention: Celebrity endorsements contribute to user acquisition and retention on play-to-earn platforms. This section explores how the star power of celebrities draws attention to virtual economies, bringing in new players and sustaining the interest of existing communities.

- Cultural Integration and Mainstream Recognition: Celebrity endorsements play a crucial role in integrating play-to-earn into mainstream culture. The chapter analyzes how endorsements from well-known figures elevate the cultural status of virtual economies, making them more accessible and acceptable to a broader audience.

Celebrity-Gamer Partnerships: Navigating Collaborative Spaces

- Collaborative Ventures Between Celebrities and Gamers: The collaboration between celebrities and professional gamers is a noteworthy trend. This section investigates partnerships where celebrities team up with renowned gamers, exploring how these alliances contribute to the evolving landscape of play-to-earn and e-sports.

- Live Streaming and Social Media Presence: Celebrities often leverage their massive social media following to engage with audiences in real-time. The chapter examines how live streaming sessions, gameplay commentary, and interactive Q&A sessions on platforms like Twitch and YouTube amplify the connection between celebrities and play-to-earn enthusiasts.

Challenges and Considerations in Celebrity Endorsements

- Authenticity and Genuine Interest: The authenticity of celebrity endorsements is a crucial aspect. This part of the chapter explores the challenges associated with ensuring that celebrities genuinely embrace and understand the play-to-earn ecosystem, maintaining credibility within the gaming community.

- Navigating the Regulatory Landscape: Celebrity endorsements in the crypto and gaming space require careful consideration of regulatory frameworks. This section delves into the challenges and legal considerations that celebrities and play-to-earn platforms face when navigating the regulatory landscape.

Fan Engagement and Community Building: The Ripple Effect

- Enhancing Fan Engagement: Celebrity endorsements enhance fan engagement within play-to-earn communities. This section examines how the involvement of celebrities sparks conversations, drives fan interactions, and creates a sense of camaraderie among players who share both gaming and celebrity interests.

- Community Building Beyond Virtual Economies: The chapter explores how celebrity endorsements contribute to community building not only within play-to-earn platforms but also across social media, forums, and other online spaces. The ripple effect of celebrity influence extends beyond virtual economies, creating interconnected communities.

Future Collaborations: The Ongoing Marriage of Celebrity and Play-to-Earn

- Anticipating Future Celebrity Collaborations: The chapter concludes by speculating on the future of celebrity endorsements in play-to-earn gaming. It explores potential collaborations, emerging trends, and the evolving role of celebrities in shaping the narrative of virtual economies in the years to come.

Conclusion: Celebrities as Catalysts for Virtual Economic Renaissance

In conclusion, celebrities like Snoop Dogg and sports stars have become catalysts, ushering play-to-earn gaming into the limelight. Their endorsements and active participation not only elevate the cultural significance of virtual economies but also create bridges between diverse audiences. The chapter highlights how celebrities, with their star power and influence, contribute to the evolving landscape of play-to-earn, transforming it from a niche interest to a global phenomenon that transcends the boundaries between entertainment, gaming, and mainstream culture.

Chapter 9 - User Experience and Accessibility
Breaking Barriers: Custodial Wallets and Fiat On-Ramps in Play-to-Earn

The democratization of play-to-earn gaming relies heavily on accessible entry points for users. This chapter explores how custodial wallets and fiat on-ramps have played pivotal roles in lowering barriers, making play-to-earn gaming more inclusive and user-friendly.

Understanding Custodial Wallets: A Gateway to the Virtual Economy

- Introduction to Custodial Wallets: This section provides an overview of custodial wallets, explaining their role as a user-friendly gateway for individuals entering the play-to-earn ecosystem. It explores how custodial wallets simplify the onboarding process, offering a familiar interface for users new to blockchain and crypto technologies.

- Security Measures and User Protections: Despite being custodial, these wallets implement robust security measures. The chapter delves into the security features of custodial wallets, reassuring users about the safety of their assets and personal information while highlighting the importance of balancing accessibility with security.

- User-Friendly Interfaces and Intuitive Designs: Custodial wallets prioritize user experience through intuitive designs and user-friendly interfaces. This part explores how these wallets leverage familiar design elements to make navigation seamless, catering to both crypto novices and experienced users.

Fiat On-Ramps: Bridging the Gap Between Traditional and Virtual Currencies

- The Role of Fiat On-Ramps: Fiat on-ramps serve as bridges between traditional currencies and the world of cryptocurrencies. This section explains how fiat on-ramps enable users to convert traditional currencies into crypto assets, facilitating entry into play-to-earn gaming without the need for extensive knowledge of crypto trading.

- Integration with Payment Methods: Exploring how fiat on-ramps seamlessly integrate with various payment methods, the chapter illustrates the simplicity with which users can fund their play-to-earn activities. Whether through credit cards, bank transfers, or other means, fiat on-ramps provide versatile options for users.

- Addressing Regulatory Compliance: Fiat on-ramps often navigate complex regulatory landscapes. This part of the chapter discusses how these platforms adhere to compliance standards, ensuring a secure and legal environment for users to transition between fiat and cryptocurrencies.

The Synergy of Custodial Wallets and Fiat On-Ramps:

- Simplified Onboarding Processes: The chapter examines how the combination of custodial wallets and fiat on-ramps streamlines the onboarding process for new users. By offering a familiar fiat-to-crypto transition, users can easily grasp the mechanics of play-to-earn gaming without the steep learning curve associated with traditional blockchain transactions.

- Reducing Cryptocurrency Complexity: Cryptocurrencies, with their intricate technicalities, can be intimidating for newcomers. This section explores how custodial wallets and fiat on-ramps simplify the cryptocurrency experience, making it more accessible and less daunting for individuals entering the play-to-earn space.

Real-World Examples and Success Stories:

- Case Studies of Successful Custodial Wallet and Fiat On-Ramp Integration: The chapter presents real-world examples of platforms that have successfully integrated custodial wallets and fiat on-ramps. Examining user adoption rates, feedback, and success stories, this section illustrates the positive impact of accessible entry points on the growth of play-to-earn ecosystems.

- User Testimonials: Featuring testimonials from users who entered the play-to-earn space through custodial wallets and fiat on-ramps, this part of the chapter provides authentic narratives of their experiences. These testimonials highlight the user-friendly nature of these entry points and the impact on their overall play-to-earn journey.

Challenges and Considerations:

- Balancing Security and Accessibility: The chapter delves into the inherent challenges of balancing security and accessibility. While custodial wallets prioritize user-friendly interfaces, maintaining robust security measures is paramount. This section discusses how platforms navigate this delicate equilibrium.

- Regulatory Challenges: Custodial wallets and fiat on-ramps often face regulatory challenges. This part explores the complexities of adhering to diverse global regulations and the impact on the accessibility of play-to-earn gaming for users in different regions.

Future Innovations and Evolutions:

- Emerging Technologies in User Onboarding: The chapter speculates on the future of user onboarding in play-to-earn gaming, exploring potential innovations in custodial wallets and fiat on-ramps. From enhanced security features to more seamless fiat-to-crypto transitions, this section envisions the evolution of entry points into virtual economies.

- Global Expansion and Inclusive Access: As play-to-earn gaming continues to gain global traction, the chapter discusses how custodial wallets and fiat on-ramps can contribute to the global expansion of virtual economies, fostering inclusive access for users worldwide.

Conclusion: Custodial Wallets and Fiat On-Ramps as Pillars of Inclusivity

In conclusion, custodial wallets and fiat on-ramps stand as crucial pillars in making play-to-earn gaming inclusive and accessible. By simplifying the user onboarding process, reducing the complexity of cryptocurrency transactions, and bridging the gap between traditional and virtual currencies, these entry points empower a diverse user base to participate in the transformative potential of play-to-earn economies. As technological advancements continue to refine user experiences, custodial wallets and fiat on-ramps will play instrumental roles in shaping the future landscape of virtual economies.

Guiding the Way: Enhancing User Onboarding in Play-to-Earn Gaming

Ensuring a seamless and informative entry into the world of play-to-earn gaming is crucial for user retention and satisfaction. This chapter explores the significance of improving new user tutorials, guides, and community support, providing an in-depth analysis of how these elements contribute to a positive and enriching user experience.

The Role of New User Tutorials: A Gateway to the Virtual Realm

- Introduction to New User Tutorials: This section establishes the fundamental importance of new user tutorials in play-to-earn gaming. It delves into the purpose of tutorials as educational tools designed to introduce players to the unique mechanics, features, and opportunities within the play-to-earn ecosystem.

- Creating Engaging and Informative Content: Exploring effective strategies for content creation, the chapter discusses how new user tutorials should balance engagement with information. It examines the use of multimedia, interactive elements, and user-friendly language to ensure that tutorials are both enjoyable and educational.

- Addressing Diverse Learning Styles: Recognizing that users have diverse learning styles, this part of the chapter explores how new user tutorials can cater to visual, auditory, and kinesthetic learners. It discusses the integration of diverse learning modalities to create a more inclusive onboarding experience.

Comprehensive Guides: Navigating the Play-to-Earn Landscape

- Importance of Comprehensive Guides: This section emphasizes the value of comprehensive guides in providing users with a deeper understanding of the play-to-earn ecosystem. It discusses how guides go beyond basic tutorials, offering in-depth insights into advanced gameplay mechanics, strategies, and potential earning avenues.

- Exploring Different Aspects of Play-to-Earn: The chapter breaks down various aspects of play-to-earn gaming that comprehensive guides should cover. From understanding tokenomics and decentralized finance (DeFi) to exploring different game genres, these guides serve as invaluable resources for users seeking a holistic grasp of the virtual economy.

- Community-Sourced Guides and User Contributions: Acknowledging the power of community collaboration, this part examines the role of user-generated guides. It explores how communities contribute to a collective knowledge base, creating guides that resonate with the experiences and insights of seasoned players.

Building a Supportive Community: Fostering Connection and Learning

- The Importance of Community Support: This section underscores the significance of community support in the onboarding process. It explores how a welcoming and informative community can significantly impact a new player's experience, providing assistance, guidance, and a sense of belonging.

- Creating Welcoming Spaces: Discussing the characteristics of inclusive online communities, the chapter examines how play-to-earn platforms can create welcoming spaces for new users. It delves into moderation strategies, community guidelines, and initiatives that foster positive interactions.

- Live Q&A Sessions and Interactive Support: The chapter explores the effectiveness of live question and answer sessions within the community. It discusses how real-time interactions, whether through forums, social media, or dedicated platforms, can enhance the learning experience for new players.

User Testimonials and Success Stories: Realizing the Impact

- Showcasing User Journeys: Highlighting the power of storytelling, this section explores the inclusion of user testimonials and success stories within onboarding materials. It discusses how real-life narratives can inspire and motivate new players, offering relatable examples of individuals who have navigated and succeeded in the play-to-earn space.

- User-Generated Content as Educational Tools: The chapter examines the role of user-generated content, such as video tutorials and written accounts, as educational tools. It explores how these authentic contributions can complement official tutorials and guides, providing a diverse range of perspectives and insights.

Challenges in Onboarding and Community Building: Navigating Obstacles

- Overcoming Language and Cultural Barriers: Acknowledging the global nature of play-to-earn communities, this part discusses the challenges associated with language and cultural differences. It explores strategies to overcome these barriers and create inclusive onboarding experiences for users from diverse backgrounds.

- Addressing Information Overload: Recognizing the potential for information overload, the chapter explores strategies to present information in a digestible and phased manner. It discusses the importance of progressive learning and the gradual introduction of complex concepts as users advance in their play-to-earn journey.

Continuous Improvement: Iterative Strategies for Enhanced Onboarding

- Feedback Loops and Iterative Updates: The chapter concludes by emphasizing the importance of feedback loops in the onboarding process. It explores how play-to-earn platforms can leverage user feedback to continuously refine and improve tutorials, guides, and community support, ensuring an evolving and adaptive onboarding experience.

Conclusion: Guiding New Explorers in the Play-to-Earn Universe

In conclusion, the chapter underscores the pivotal role of new user tutorials, comprehensive guides, and community support in shaping a positive onboarding experience for play-to-earn gaming enthusiasts. By fostering engaging and informative entry points, platforms can empower users to navigate the complexities of virtual economies, build connections within communities, and embark on fulfilling journeys within the play-to-earn universe. As play-to-earn gaming continues to evolve, the ongoing enhancement of onboarding strategies will be essential in nurturing a thriving and inclusive ecosystem.

Mobile Empowerment: Play-to-Earn On the Go

This chapter explores the transformative impact of mobile apps and lite clients on the accessibility and user experience within the play-to-earn gaming ecosystem. By delving into the development, advantages, challenges, and potential future advancements of mobile applications and lite clients, the narrative unfolds how these innovations contribute to the evolution of play-to-earn gaming.

The Mobile Revolution in Play-to-Earn Gaming: An Overview

- Introduction to Mobile Apps and Lite Clients: This section provides a foundational understanding of mobile applications and lite clients in the context of play-to-earn gaming. It explores the evolution of these technologies and their role in reshaping the accessibility and convenience of participating in virtual economies.

- Advantages of Mobile Access: The chapter outlines the unique advantages that mobile access brings to play-to-earn gaming. From flexibility and convenience to the potential for increased user engagement, it highlights how mobile applications enable users to seamlessly integrate play-to-earn activities into their daily lives.

Development and Design Considerations: Crafting a Seamless Mobile Experience

- User Interface and Experience (UI/UX) Design: Delving into the specifics of design, this section explores how UI/UX considerations play a pivotal role in the development of effective mobile apps and lite clients. It discusses the importance of intuitive interfaces, simplified navigation, and user-friendly features that cater to a diverse user base.

- Scalability Challenges and Solutions: Acknowledging the scalability challenges inherent in mobile platforms, the chapter examines how developers address these issues. It explores solutions such as optimized coding practices, server-side enhancements, and the integration of scalable infrastructure to ensure a smooth and responsive experience for users.

- Cross-Platform Compatibility: Recognizing the diversity of devices and operating systems in the mobile landscape, the chapter discusses the importance of cross-platform compatibility. It explores how developers strive to create applications that seamlessly function across various devices, ensuring a consistent experience for users regardless of their chosen platform.

Security and Trust: Safeguarding User Assets in the Mobile Realm

- Ensuring Asset Security: Security is paramount in play-to-earn gaming, and this section explores the measures taken to secure user assets within mobile applications. It discusses encryption, two-factor authentication, and other security protocols implemented to safeguard players' digital possessions.

- Addressing Trust Concerns: Acknowledging user concerns about trust and security in mobile play-to-earn environments, the chapter explores strategies to build trust. It discusses transparent communication, adherence to industry standards, and the role of community feedback in fostering a trustworthy mobile gaming ecosystem.

Enhanced Accessibility: Lite Clients and Their Impact

- Lite Clients: Definition and Purpose: The chapter introduces lite clients and their role in enhancing accessibility. It discusses how lite clients offer a streamlined, lightweight alternative for users with limited device capabilities or those seeking a more resource-efficient option.

- Data Usage Considerations: Recognizing the potential constraints of mobile data usage, this part explores how lite clients minimize data consumption. It discusses optimizations in data transfer, caching mechanisms, and other strategies that contribute to a more data-friendly play-to-earn experience.

- Offline Functionality: Exploring the concept of offline functionality within lite clients, the chapter examines how these clients allow users to engage in play-to-earn activities even in the absence of a consistent internet connection. It discusses the implications of offline functionality on user engagement and accessibility.

Real-World Implementation: Success Stories and User Experiences

- Case Studies of Successful Mobile Apps: This section showcases real-world examples of successful play-to-earn mobile applications. It explores user adoption rates, positive feedback, and the impact of these applications on the overall growth of play-to-earn ecosystems.

- User Testimonials: Featuring testimonials from users who have embraced play-to-earn mobile apps, this part provides authentic narratives of their experiences. It highlights the seamless integration of play-to-earn gaming into users' daily lives and the positive impact on their overall gaming experience.

Challenges and Future Prospects: Navigating the Mobile Frontier

- Device Fragmentation Challenges: Acknowledging the diversity of mobile devices, this section explores the challenges associated with device fragmentation. It discusses how developers navigate this landscape to ensure a consistent and enjoyable experience for users across a wide range of devices.

- Emerging Technologies and Future Innovations: The chapter concludes by speculating on the future of mobile apps and lite clients in play-to-earn gaming. It explores potential technological advancements, innovations, and trends that may further enhance the accessibility and user experience within the mobile gaming space.

Conclusion: Empowering Players On the Move

In conclusion, the chapter underscores the transformative role of mobile apps and lite clients in play-to-earn gaming. By providing users with convenient, accessible, and secure ways to engage in virtual economies, these technologies contribute significantly to the democratization of play-to-earn activities. As advancements continue, the ongoing development and refinement of mobile applications and lite clients will play a pivotal role in shaping the future landscape of play-to-earn gaming, offering users unprecedented flexibility and freedom to participate in virtual economies whenever and wherever they choose.

The Impact of UX and Visual Design Enhancements

This chapter delves into the critical role of user experience (UX) and visual design enhancements in shaping the play-to-earn gaming landscape. By exploring the symbiotic relationship between effective UX design and visually engaging interfaces, the narrative unfolds the strategies, principles, and innovations that elevate the overall gaming experience for participants in virtual economies.

Foundations of User Experience in Play-to-Earn Gaming

- Introduction to User Experience (UX): Establishing a foundational understanding, this section defines the concept of UX in the context of play-to-earn gaming. It delves into the significance of creating positive, intuitive, and enjoyable interactions for players engaging with decentralized virtual economies.

- The Psychological Aspect of Gaming: Examining the psychological elements that contribute to a compelling UX, this part explores how design choices impact player emotions, motivations, and overall satisfaction. It discusses the intersection of game mechanics, rewards, and user engagement in fostering an immersive gaming experience.

- User-Centric Design Principles: Introducing user-centric design principles, the chapter discusses the importance of placing players at the center of the design process. It explores concepts such as usability, accessibility, and inclusivity, emphasizing the need for interfaces that cater to diverse player demographics.

Visual Design in Play-to-Earn: Beyond Aesthetics

- The Role of Visual Design: This section outlines the multifaceted role of visual design in play-to-earn gaming. It discusses how aesthetics, color schemes, and visual elements contribute to creating memorable and impactful gaming environments.

- Branding and Consistency: Exploring the branding strategies employed in play-to-earn platforms, the chapter examines how consistent visual design builds a cohesive and recognizable identity. It delves into the importance of creating a visual language that resonates with the platform's values and user expectations.

- Immersive Environments and Virtual Worlds: Focusing on the creation of immersive virtual worlds, this part explores how visual design enhances the sense of presence and engagement for players. It discusses the use of graphics, animations, and other visual elements to transport players into dynamic and captivating gaming environments.

Strategies for Effective UX Design in Play-to-Earn

- Onboarding and Tutorials: Delving into the onboarding process, the chapter explores UX design strategies for effective tutorials. It discusses the seamless integration of educational elements, interactive guides, and intuitive interfaces to ensure a smooth entry for new players.

- Navigation and Information Hierarchy: Examining the importance of intuitive navigation, the section explores how UX design establishes clear information hierarchies. It discusses the strategic placement of essential information, menus, and controls to facilitate effortless navigation within play-to-earn platforms.

- Feedback Mechanisms: Recognizing the significance of feedback in player engagement, this part explores UX design strategies for providing meaningful feedback. It discusses visual cues, notifications, and responsive interfaces that keep players informed about their actions, progress, and in-game events.

Innovations in Play-to-Earn UX:

- Gamification Elements: This section explores the integration of gamification elements into UX design. It discusses how features such as leaderboards, achievements, and interactive challenges contribute to a more engaging and rewarding play-to-earn experience.

- Personalization and Customization: Acknowledging the diversity of player preferences, the chapter examines UX design innovations that allow for personalization and customization. It discusses the implementation of customizable avatars, in-game assets, and preferences to enhance player agency and connection.

- Dynamic User Interfaces (UI): Exploring the concept of dynamic UI, this part discusses how UX design adapts to user behavior and preferences. It explores the use of responsive interfaces that evolve based on player actions, creating a dynamic and personalized gaming experience.

Accessibility and Inclusivity: Designing for All Players

- Ensuring Accessibility: This section explores UX design strategies for ensuring accessibility in play-to-earn gaming. It discusses considerations for players with diverse abilities and the implementation of features such as text-to-speech, subtitles, and adjustable settings.

- Inclusive Design Practices: Examining inclusive design practices, the chapter explores how UX design can accommodate players from various demographics. It discusses considerations for diverse cultural backgrounds, age groups, and user preferences in creating universally accessible play-to-earn experiences.

Testing and Iteration: The Continuous Refinement of UX

- The Role of User Testing: Highlighting the importance of user testing, this section explores how play-to-earn platforms conduct iterative testing to gather player feedback. It discusses the insights gained from real user experiences and the role of feedback loops in refining UX design.

- Agile Development and Continuous Improvement: Exploring the principles of agile development, the chapter discusses how play-to-earn platforms embrace continuous improvement in UX design. It examines the iterative nature of development cycles, allowing for swift adaptations based on user input and evolving industry trends.

Challenges and Solutions: Navigating the UX Design Landscape

- Balancing Complexity and Simplicity: Acknowledging the challenges of balancing complexity and simplicity in play-to-earn UX design, this part explores strategies to create interfaces that cater to both novice and experienced players. It discusses the potential pitfalls of overwhelming users with information and the importance of gradual learning curves.

- Cross-Platform Consistency: Recognizing the prevalence of cross-platform gaming, the chapter discusses the challenges of maintaining consistent UX across various devices. It explores solutions to ensure a seamless experience for players transitioning between desktop, mobile, and other platforms.

Conclusion: Elevating the Play-to-Earn Experience Through Design

In conclusion, the chapter underscores the pivotal role of UX and visual design enhancements in shaping the play-to-earn gaming experience. By prioritizing user-centric design, incorporating visual elements that evoke emotions, and embracing innovations that cater to diverse player preferences, play-to-earn platforms can create immersive and memorable gaming environments. As the industry continues to evolve, the ongoing refinement of UX design will be instrumental in fostering player engagement, accessibility, and the overall success of play-to-earn ecosystems.

Localization and translation for Global Audiences

This chapter explores the intricate world of localization and translation within the context of play-to-earn gaming. Delving into the nuanced process of adapting games for diverse linguistic and cultural audiences, the narrative unravels the strategies, challenges, and impact of ensuring a globally inclusive experience for players in decentralized virtual economies.

Understanding the Importance of Localization and Translation

- Introduction to Localization: Establishing a foundational understanding, this section defines localization in the context of play-to-earn gaming. It explores how the process goes beyond mere translation, encompassing cultural adaptation, regional nuances, and the creation of an immersive, culturally resonant experience for players.

- The Multifaceted Role of Translation: Examining the critical role of translation, the chapter discusses how linguistic accuracy and cultural context preservation are vital for effective communication within play-to-earn platforms. It explores the intricacies of conveying complex game mechanics, narratives, and community interactions across diverse languages.

Cultural Sensitivity and Adaptation in Play-to-Earn Games

- Cultural Nuances in Gaming: This section delves into the diverse cultural landscapes that play-to-earn games navigate. It discusses the significance of understanding cultural nuances, traditions, and sensitivities to create content that resonates positively with players from different backgrounds.

- Adapting Narratives and Themes: Exploring the adaptation of game narratives and themes, the chapter discusses how localization extends beyond language to encompass the contextualization of storylines, characters, and in-game events. It highlights the impact of culturally relevant narratives in fostering player engagement.

- Inclusive Representation: Recognizing the importance of inclusive representation, this part explores how localization contributes to diverse character portrayals and representation within play-to-earn games. It discusses the adaptation of characters, avatars, and in-game assets to reflect the global player base.

Strategies for Effective Localization and Translation

- Collaboration with Local Experts: This section explores the value of collaborating with local experts, linguists, and cultural consultants during the localization process. It discusses how partnerships with individuals familiar with regional nuances contribute to accurate and culturally sensitive adaptations.

- Dynamic Translation Tools and Technologies: Examining the role of technology, the chapter discusses dynamic translation tools that enhance the efficiency and accuracy of localization efforts. It explores machine translation, artificial intelligence, and other technologies that support the rapid adaptation of content across multiple languages.

- Iterative Feedback Loops: Highlighting the importance of iterative feedback loops, this part discusses how play-to-earn platforms incorporate player feedback during and after localization. It explores strategies for gathering insights from diverse player communities to refine and improve localized content.

Overcoming Challenges in Localization and Translation

- Maintaining Consistency Across Languages: Acknowledging the challenge of maintaining consistency, the chapter explores strategies to ensure uniformity in gameplay experiences across different language versions. It discusses the potential pitfalls of divergence in tone, terminology, and user experience.

- Navigating Linguistic Diversity: Recognizing the linguistic diversity of the global player base, this section explores how play-to-earn platforms navigate challenges related to dialects, regional variations, and linguistic preferences. It discusses strategies to create adaptable localization frameworks that cater to a broad spectrum of linguistic nuances.

- Addressing Cultural Sensitivities: Delving into the delicate balance required in addressing cultural sensitivities, the chapter examines strategies for avoiding cultural misunderstandings or unintentional offense during the localization process. It discusses the importance of cultural awareness training for localization teams.

Success Stories in Play-to-Earn Localization

- Case Studies of Effective Localization: This part showcases real-world examples of play-to-earn games that have successfully navigated the challenges of localization. It explores instances where effective cultural adaptation and translation strategies have contributed to increased player engagement, positive community feedback, and global success.

- Community Involvement in Localization: Examining the role of community involvement, the chapter discusses how play-to-earn platforms leverage the support and input of the player community during the localization process. It explores strategies for fostering collaborative efforts that enhance the authenticity and effectiveness of localized content.

The Impact of Localization on Player Engagement

- Community Building Through Localization: This section explores how localization contributes to community building within play-to-earn platforms. It discusses the role of shared cultural references, language-specific events, and localized community engagement initiatives in fostering a sense of belonging among players.

- Increased User Retention and Monetization: Examining the business impact, the chapter discusses how effective localization positively influences user retention and monetization. It explores how players are more likely to engage with, invest in, and remain loyal to platforms that cater to their linguistic and cultural preferences.

Emerging Trends in Play-to-Earn Localization

- Real-Time Dynamic Localization: Exploring the potential of real-time dynamic localization, this section discusses emerging trends that aim to provide seamless and continuously updated translations as games evolve. It examines the use of AI-driven tools and adaptive localization frameworks to enhance player experiences.

- Customizable Language Settings: Recognizing player preferences, the chapter explores the concept of customizable language settings within play-to-earn games. It discusses the implementation of user-friendly interfaces that allow players to personalize their language experience, enhancing accessibility and comfort.

Conclusion: Nurturing a Global Gaming Community Through Localization

In conclusion, the chapter emphasizes the integral role of localization and translation in fostering a global gaming community within play-to-earn platforms. By embracing cultural diversity, linguistic inclusivity, and player collaboration, these platforms can create an environment where players from around the world feel not just accommodated, but truly immersed in a gaming experience tailored to their unique preferences and backgrounds. As play-to-earn gaming continues to evolve, the ongoing commitment to effective localization will be paramount in ensuring the sustained growth, inclusivity, and success of decentralized virtual economies on a global scale.

Chapter 10 - The Future of Play-to-Earn Gaming
Envisioning Billions of Mainstream, Casual Gamers in the Future

This chapter delves into the transformative potential of play-to-earn gaming as it extends its reach to billions of mainstream, casual gamers worldwide. Exploring the factors that can drive mass adoption, the narrative envisions a future where decentralized virtual economies redefine the gaming landscape, making play-to-earn accessible and appealing to a global audience.

Mainstreaming Play-to-Earn: A Paradigm Shift

- From Niche to Mainstream: This section explores the evolution of play-to-earn gaming from a niche market to a mainstream phenomenon. It delves into the factors that have contributed to the gradual acceptance of decentralized virtual economies by the broader gaming community.

- Democratization of Gaming Income: Examining the democratization of gaming income, the chapter discusses how play-to-earn models provide opportunities for players of all skill levels to earn rewards. It explores the appeal of decentralized virtual economies as a means for mainstream gamers to monetize their leisure time.

- The Allure of Earning While Playing: This part explores the psychological appeal of earning real value while engaging in gaming for mainstream and casual players. It delves into how the prospect of tangible rewards can draw a wider audience, transcending the traditional boundaries between gaming and economic participation.

Breaking Down Barriers to Entry

- Simplified Onboarding Processes: This section discusses the importance of streamlined onboarding processes to attract mainstream and casual gamers. It explores strategies to simplify the initial entry into play-to-earn ecosystems, ensuring a user-friendly experience for individuals unfamiliar with blockchain technology.

- Custodial Wallets and Fiat On-Ramps: Examining the role of custodial wallets and fiat on-ramps, the chapter explores how these tools lower barriers to entry for mainstream players. It discusses the importance of providing accessible avenues for acquiring and managing digital assets without the complexities of cryptocurrency exchanges.

- User-Friendly Tutorials and Support: This part explores the significance of user-friendly tutorials and robust community support mechanisms. It discusses how comprehensive guides and responsive communities can empower mainstream and casual gamers to navigate play-to-earn platforms with confidence.

The Appeal to Casual Gamers: Balancing Fun and Earnings

- Casual-Friendly Gameplay Mechanics: This section delves into the importance of developing casual-friendly gameplay mechanics within play-to-earn games. It explores how incorporating intuitive, easy-to-understand gameplay can attract a broader audience beyond dedicated gamers.

- Engaging Storylines and Genres: Examining the role of engaging storylines and diverse genres, the chapter discusses how play-to-earn platforms can appeal to casual gamers through narratives that resonate with a wide range of interests. It explores the potential of introducing various game genres beyond traditional gaming boundaries.

- Dynamic Balance Between Playability and Earnings: This part explores the delicate balance between playability and earnings potential. It discusses how play-to-earn games can optimize this equilibrium to keep casual players engaged without compromising the fundamental economic principles of the decentralized ecosystem.

Mobile Integration: Gaming on the Go

- The Rise of Mobile Play-to-Earn: This section explores the increasing significance of mobile play-to-earn experiences. It discusses how the accessibility and convenience of mobile devices can bring play-to-earn gaming to mainstream audiences, allowing them to participate seamlessly in decentralized virtual economies.

- Lite Clients for Easy Access: Examining the development of lite clients, the chapter explores how these streamlined versions of play-to-earn platforms enhance accessibility for casual gamers on mobile devices. It discusses the importance of minimizing data and resource requirements for a smooth mobile gaming experience.

Global Appeal: Localized Experiences

- Localization for Diverse Cultures: This part explores the role of localization in making play-to-earn gaming globally appealing. It discusses strategies for tailoring in-game content, language, and cultural references to resonate with diverse audiences, ensuring that mainstream and casual gamers feel a sense of inclusivity.

- Inclusive Representation in Games: Examining the importance of inclusive representation, the chapter explores how play-to-earn games can attract a global audience by featuring diverse characters and themes. It discusses the impact of representation on player engagement and the creation of a welcoming gaming environment.

Innovations Driving Mainstream Adoption

- Virtual Reality and Augmented Reality Integration: This section explores the potential integration of virtual reality (VR) and augmented reality (AR) in play-to-earn gaming. It discusses how immersive experiences can captivate mainstream audiences and contribute to the evolution of play-to-earn into a multi-sensory, interactive phenomenon.

- Cross-Platform Interoperability: Examining cross-platform interoperability, the chapter explores how the seamless transition of in-game assets and progress across various platforms can attract mainstream gamers. It discusses the importance of breaking down silos between different gaming ecosystems to create a unified and user-friendly experience.

The Role of Influencers, Celebrities, and Media

- Influencer Endorsements: This part explores the role of influencers in bridging the gap between play-to-earn gaming and mainstream audiences. It discusses how influencers can introduce decentralized virtual economies to their followers, adding credibility and familiarity to these emerging platforms.

- Celebrity Endorsements and Collaborations: Examining the impact of celebrity endorsements, the chapter discusses how partnerships with well-known figures can elevate the visibility of play-to-earn gaming. It explores how endorsements from celebrities in entertainment, sports, and other industries can bring decentralized virtual economies into the mainstream spotlight.

- Media Coverage and Educational Initiatives: This section delves into the significance of media coverage and educational initiatives in raising awareness about play-to-earn gaming. It discusses the role of documentaries, news features, and educational campaigns in demystifying decentralized virtual economies for mainstream audiences.

Challenges on the Path to Mainstream Adoption

- Educational Hurdles: This part explores the educational challenges associated with bringing play-to-earn gaming to mainstream audiences. It discusses the need for comprehensive educational initiatives to inform casual gamers about blockchain technology, digital assets, and the potential of decentralized virtual economies.

- Regulatory Considerations: Examining regulatory considerations, the chapter discusses the potential impact of evolving regulations on the mainstream adoption of play-to-earn gaming. It explores how transparent and compliant platforms can build trust and credibility, assuaging concerns among mainstream users.

Conclusion: Paving the Way for Billions of Play-to-Earn Enthusiasts

In conclusion, the chapter envisions a future where play-to-earn gaming transcends its current niche and becomes a global phenomenon embraced by billions of mainstream and casual players. By focusing on accessibility, engaging gameplay, mobile integration, global appeal through localization, and leveraging influencers and media, play-to-earn platforms can overcome barriers and redefine the gaming landscape. As the industry continues to evolve, the collaboration between blockchain technology, gaming innovation, and mainstream adoption will shape a new era where play-to-earn becomes a ubiquitous and transformative part of the gaming experience for individuals around the world.

Exploring the Future of Play-to-Earn with VR/AR Integration and New Gaming Genres

This chapter delves into the revolutionary convergence of play-to-earn gaming with cutting-edge technologies, specifically Virtual Reality (VR) and Augmented Reality (AR). Unveiling the potential of immersive experiences and the emergence of new gaming genres, the narrative explores how VR/AR integrated play-to-earn is poised to redefine the gaming landscape and reshape the dynamics of decentralized virtual economies.

The Rise of Immersive Experiences: A Paradigm Shift in Gaming

- Introduction to VR and AR Integration: This section provides an overview of the transformative integration of VR and AR technologies into play-to-earn gaming. It discusses how these technologies extend beyond traditional screens, immersing players in virtual worlds where they can interact with digital assets and earn rewards in ways previously unimaginable.

- Immersive Gameplay Mechanics: Examining the impact of immersive gameplay mechanics, the chapter explores how VR and AR redefine the way players engage with play-to-earn environments. It discusses the incorporation of gesture controls, spatial awareness, and real-world interactions to enhance the overall gaming experience and economic participation.

Exploring New Dimensions: VR/AR-Driven Gaming Genres

- VR-Integrated Role-Playing Games (RPGs): This part delves into the evolution of RPGs within VR environments. It explores how players can immerse themselves in rich, narrative-driven experiences where in-game actions have tangible economic consequences, allowing for a deeper integration of play-to-earn dynamics.

- AR-Enhanced Strategy Games: Examining the fusion of AR with strategy games, the chapter discusses how players can overlay digital elements onto the real world, creating dynamic and interactive environments. It explores the potential for strategic decision-making to directly impact economic outcomes within play-to-earn ecosystems.

- Immersive Simulation Environments: This section explores the creation of immersive simulation environments using VR technology. It discusses how players can engage in realistic scenarios where economic decisions and actions within the virtual space translate into tangible rewards, creating a novel dimension for play-to-earn gaming.

The Economic Landscape of VR/AR-Integrated Play-to-Earn

- Asset Ownership in Virtual Worlds: This part discusses the concept of asset ownership within VR/AR-integrated play-to-earn environments. It explores how players can truly own and interact with digital assets in virtual spaces, creating a sense of ownership that extends beyond traditional gaming experiences.

- Economic Impact of Real-Time VR Transactions: Examining the real-time nature of VR transactions, the chapter explores how economic activities within virtual environments can occur seamlessly and instantly. It discusses the potential for immediate rewards tied to in-game actions, fostering a dynamic and responsive play-to-earn ecosystem.

- Integration with Blockchain and Smart Contracts: This section discusses the integration of blockchain technology and smart contracts within VR/AR play-to-earn environments. It explores how these technologies enhance security, transparency, and trust, allowing for verifiable ownership of digital assets and streamlined economic interactions.

Challenges and Opportunities in VR/AR Play-to-Earn

- Technological Hurdles: This part explores the technological challenges associated with VR/AR integration in play-to-earn gaming. It discusses issues such as hardware requirements, accessibility, and the need for continuous innovation to overcome barriers to entry for players.

- Ensuring Inclusivity in Immersive Experiences: Examining the importance of inclusivity, the chapter discusses how VR/AR play-to-earn platforms can ensure that immersive experiences cater to a diverse global audience. It explores strategies for overcoming potential exclusionary factors and fostering a broad user base.

- Balancing Immersion with Accessibility: This section delves into the delicate balance between immersive experiences and accessibility within VR/AR play-to-earn. It discusses how platforms can create environments that captivate players while maintaining user-friendly interfaces and intuitive mechanics.

Community Building and Social Interaction in VR/AR Environments

- Virtual Guilds and Communities: This part explores the potential for virtual guilds and communities within VR environments. It discusses how players can form social connections, collaborate on economic activities, and collectively shape the play-to-earn ecosystem within these immersive spaces.

- Real-World Events and Meetups: Examining the extension of play-to-earn experiences beyond virtual worlds, the chapter discusses the potential for real-world events and meetups facilitated by VR/AR technology. It explores how players can engage in economic activities both in virtual and physical spaces.

- Social Trading and Economic Collaboration: This section explores the concept of social trading and economic collaboration within VR/AR play-to-earn environments. It discusses how players can leverage social networks to enhance their economic strategies, share insights, and collectively navigate decentralized virtual economies.

The Evolution of Ownership and Governance in VR/AR Play-to-Earn

- Decentralized Governance Structures: This part discusses the evolution of decentralized governance structures within VR/AR play-to-earn ecosystems. It explores how blockchain technology enables community-driven decision-making, shaping the rules and governance mechanisms of virtual economies.

- User-Generated Content and Creativity: Examining the role of user-generated content, the chapter explores how VR/AR play-to-earn platforms empower players to contribute creatively to the virtual environment. It discusses the economic implications of user-generated assets and experiences within these immersive spaces.

Innovations Shaping the Future: VR/AR-Driven Play-to-Earn Trends

- Dynamic Environments and Seasonal Changes: This section explores the potential for dynamic virtual environments and seasonal changes within VR/AR play-to-earn. It discusses how the integration of real-world events, weather patterns, and seasonal shifts can create diverse economic opportunities for players.

- Cross-Platform Integration with Traditional Gaming: Examining cross-platform integration, the chapter discusses how VR/AR play-to-earn can seamlessly connect with traditional gaming experiences. It explores the potential for players to transition between different platforms while maintaining a unified economic presence.

Conclusion: Pioneering a New Era of Play-to-Earn Immersion

In conclusion, the chapter envisions a future where VR/AR integration fundamentally transforms play-to-earn gaming, offering players immersive experiences that extend beyond the confines of traditional screens. The convergence of cutting-edge technologies, new gaming genres, and economic participation within virtual worlds heralds a new era of play-to-earn innovation. As VR and AR continue to advance, the possibilities for creating vibrant, interactive, and economically thriving virtual ecosystems are limitless. The chapter invites readers to envision and participate in the unfolding narrative of VR/AR-integrated play-to-earn, where the boundaries between the virtual and real blur, and economic opportunities become boundless.

The Promise of Interoperability in Play-to-Earn Gaming's Metaverse Evolution

This chapter delves into the transformative concept of interoperability, exploring how it shapes the future of play-to-earn gaming by connecting diverse metaverse worlds and games. By breaking down the barriers between virtual realms, this narrative envisions a seamless, interconnected metaverse where players can navigate, trade, and thrive across different gaming ecosystems, fostering a new era of economic collaboration and innovation.

Understanding Interoperability in the Metaverse

- Defining Interoperability in Gaming: This section provides a comprehensive definition of interoperability in the context of play-to-earn gaming. It explores how this concept enables the seamless exchange of assets, data, and experiences across different metaverse worlds and games, creating a unified virtual ecosystem.

- The Evolution of Metaverse Connectivity: Examining the historical progression of metaverse connectivity, the chapter traces the development of interoperability from its early stages to the sophisticated, cross-platform systems that define the contemporary play-to-earn landscape.

The Economic Implications of Interconnected Metaverse Worlds

- Unified Economies and Shared Resources: This part delves into how interoperability facilitates the creation of unified economies. It discusses the economic implications of shared resources, common currencies, and standardized asset exchange protocols, fostering a collaborative environment for economic growth.

- Cross-Metaverse Trading and Asset Exchange: Examining the potential for cross-metaverse trading, the chapter explores how players can seamlessly exchange assets across different virtual worlds. It discusses the economic opportunities and challenges associated with a decentralized marketplace that transcends individual metaverse boundaries.

- Interconnected Player Professions: This section explores how interoperability transforms player professions into cross-metaverse occupations. It discusses the concept of players engaging in economic activities that span multiple virtual worlds, contributing to the emergence of cross-metaverse careers and professions.

Technological Foundations of Interoperability

- Blockchain's Role in Cross-Metaverse Connectivity: This part delves into the role of blockchain technology as the foundational layer for cross-metaverse interoperability. It discusses how blockchain enables secure, transparent, and trustless transactions, fostering a unified economic infrastructure across diverse gaming ecosystems.

- Smart Contracts and Cross-Metaverse Agreements: Examining the role of smart contracts, the chapter explores how these self-executing contracts facilitate cross-metaverse agreements. It discusses how programmable contracts automate economic interactions, ensuring that transactions and agreements are seamlessly executed across metaverse worlds.

- Decentralized Identity and Asset Ownership: This section explores the concept of decentralized identity and ownership within interconnected metaverse worlds. It discusses how blockchain technology empowers players to have verifiable ownership of digital assets, transcending individual metaverse boundaries.

Navigating the Crossroads: Challenges and Opportunities

- Technical Challenges in Cross-Metaverse Integration: This part discusses the technical challenges associated with achieving seamless interoperability. It explores issues such as different blockchain protocols, consensus mechanisms, and scalability concerns, and discusses ongoing efforts to address these challenges.

- Ensuring Economic Fairness and Stability: Examining the importance of economic fairness, the chapter discusses how interoperability introduces new considerations for maintaining stable and equitable economies across interconnected metaverse worlds. It explores strategies to prevent economic imbalances and ensure a level playing field for all participants.

- Regulatory Considerations in Cross-Metaverse Transactions: This section delves into the regulatory considerations surrounding cross-metaverse transactions. It explores the potential challenges and opportunities for regulatory frameworks to adapt to the decentralized and cross-border nature of interconnected metaverse economies.

The Social Dynamics of Interconnected Metaverse Communities

- Cultural Exchange and Diversity: This part explores how interoperability fosters cultural exchange and diversity within metaverse communities. It discusses the potential for players from different backgrounds and regions to engage in shared experiences, contributing to the creation of a global metaverse culture.

- Collaborative Gameplay Across Worlds: Examining collaborative gameplay, the chapter discusses how interoperability enables players to engage in shared quests, challenges, and adventures that span multiple metaverse worlds. It explores the social dynamics of players collaborating on a global scale.

- Emergence of Cross-Metaverse Events and Festivals: This section envisions the emergence of cross-metaverse events and festivals. It explores how interoperability allows for the organization of large-scale, collaborative gatherings within the metaverse, fostering a sense of community and shared experiences.

Interconnected Virtual Realms and Real-World Impact

- Real-World Economic Opportunities: This part discusses how interconnected metaverse economies create real-world economic opportunities. It explores the potential for players to leverage their in-game achievements and assets for various real-world applications, from education to professional development.

- Entrepreneurship and Innovation in the Metaverse: Examining the entrepreneurial aspects of the metaverse, the chapter discusses how interoperability fosters innovation and entrepreneurship. It explores how players can create and monetize unique experiences, services, and products that transcend individual metaverse boundaries.

- Influence on Traditional Industries: This section explores the impact of interconnected metaverse economies on traditional industries. It discusses how the integration of play-to-earn dynamics influences sectors such as finance, entertainment, and education, creating new opportunities and challenges for traditional businesses.

Looking Ahead: The Future of Interconnected Metaverse Economies

- Technological Advancements and Continuous Innovation: This part explores the ongoing technological advancements and innovations shaping the future of interconnected metaverse economies. It discusses how advancements in blockchain technology, artificial intelligence, and virtual reality contribute to the evolution of cross-metaverse connectivity.

- Community-Driven Development and Governance: Examining the role of community-driven development, the chapter discusses how players actively contribute to the evolution and governance of interconnected metaverse economies. It explores decentralized decision-making processes and the role of player communities in shaping the future of the metaverse.

Conclusion: Navigating the Infinite Possibilities of an Interconnected Metaverse

In conclusion, this chapter envisions a future where interoperability revolutionizes the landscape of play-to-earn gaming, creating a dynamic and interconnected metaverse where players navigate seamlessly across diverse virtual realms. The potential for unified economies, cross-metaverse collaboration, and real-world impact presents a paradigm shift in how we perceive and engage with virtual environments. As the metaverse continues to evolve, the possibilities for economic collaboration and innovation across interconnected worlds are boundless. The chapter encourages readers to explore, participate, and envision the infinite possibilities that an interconnected metaverse offers, where the lines between virtual and real become increasingly blurred, and the concept of a unified, global gaming ecosystem becomes a tangible reality.

The Rise of User-Generated Content and Creator Economies in Play-to-Earn Gaming

This chapter explores the transformative power of user-generated content (UGC) and the emergence of creator economies within the play-to-earn gaming ecosystem. From the genesis of player-driven content to the economic opportunities for creators, this narrative navigates through the evolving landscape where players become content creators, blurring the lines between consumers and producers in the dynamic world of play-to-earn.

The Birth of Player-Driven Creation

- Understanding User-Generated Content (UGC): This section defines UGC within the context of play-to-earn gaming, exploring how players contribute to the development of in-game assets, narratives, and experiences. It traces the origins of player-driven creation, highlighting early examples that paved the way for the explosion of UGC in gaming.

- Evolution of Player Creativity: Examining the evolution of player creativity, the chapter explores how advancements in technology, game design tools, and collaborative platforms have empowered players to express their creativity within virtual worlds. It discusses the shift from passive gamers to active contributors in the gaming creation process.

- UGC Platforms and Communities: This part explores the role of dedicated UGC platforms and communities that facilitate the sharing and distribution of player-created content. It discusses how these platforms have become hubs for collaboration, feedback, and the showcasing of innovative player-generated creations.

The Economic Dynamics of Creator Economies

- Monetizing Player Creativity: This section delves into the various ways players can monetize their creative contributions within play-to-earn gaming. It explores direct monetization models, such as the sale of player-created assets and content, as well as indirect models, like tips, donations, and participation in virtual economies.

- Emergence of Creator Tokens: Examining the emergence of creator tokens, the chapter discusses how blockchain technology has facilitated the creation of unique tokens tied to individual creators. It explores how these tokens can be used to reward, incentivize, and engage with the audience, forming the foundation of creator economies.

- Collaborative Economic Models: This part explores collaborative economic models where players and creators work together to share the economic benefits of player-generated content. It discusses profit-sharing mechanisms, royalties, and decentralized autonomous organizations (DAOs) that empower creators to actively participate in the economic success of their creations.

Content Creation Tools and Platforms

- Accessible Design Tools: This section discusses the importance of accessible design tools that enable players with varying levels of technical expertise to create content. It explores the evolution of user-friendly interfaces, drag-and-drop design elements, and intuitive creation tools that democratize content creation in play-to-earn gaming.

- Integration with Existing Platforms: Examining the integration of UGC tools with existing gaming platforms, the chapter discusses how major play-to-earn games incorporate and support player-created content. It explores the collaboration between game developers and players in shaping the direction of games through user-generated assets and experiences.

- Blockchain and Digital Ownership: This part explores how blockchain technology enhances digital ownership within creator economies. It discusses the use of non-fungible tokens (NFTs) to represent and authenticate player-created assets, providing a decentralized and transparent system for tracking ownership and transactions.

Challenges and Opportunities in Creator Economies

- Intellectual Property and Ownership Rights: This section addresses the challenges and opportunities related to intellectual property and ownership rights in creator economies. It explores the need for clear guidelines, smart contracts, and decentralized governance structures to ensure fair compensation and recognition for creators.

- Quality Control and Curation: Examining the issue of quality control, the chapter discusses the balance between fostering creativity and maintaining a high standard of content within play-to-earn games. It explores mechanisms for curation, user reviews, and community-driven evaluation to uphold the overall quality of player-generated content.

- Ensuring Inclusivity and Diversity: This part explores strategies to ensure inclusivity and diversity within creator economies. It discusses the importance of fostering an environment where creators from diverse backgrounds and perspectives can thrive, contributing to a rich tapestry of player-generated content.

Social and Cultural Impact of Player-Created Content

- Community Building Through UGC: This section explores how UGC contributes to community building within play-to-earn gaming. It discusses how shared creations, collaborative projects, and communal experiences enhance social interactions and strengthen the bonds among players and creators.

- Cultural Expression and Representation: Examining the cultural impact of player-created content, the chapter discusses how UGC allows for diverse cultural expressions and representations within virtual worlds. It explores how players can infuse their unique cultural influences into games, contributing to a more inclusive and culturally rich gaming landscape.

- Player-Driven Narratives and Emergent Storytelling: This part delves into the emergence of player-driven narratives and emergent storytelling within play-to-earn gaming. It discusses how UGC enables players to actively shape the stories and lore of virtual worlds, creating dynamic and evolving narratives that engage the broader player community.

Future Trends and Innovations in Creator Economies

- AI-Assisted Content Creation: This section explores the potential role of artificial intelligence (AI) in assisting content creation within play-to-earn gaming. It discusses how AI tools can augment player creativity, automate certain aspects of content creation, and contribute to the overall richness of player-generated content.

- Integration with the Metaverse: Examining the integration of UGC with the metaverse, the chapter discusses how player-created content becomes an integral part of the larger virtual ecosystem. It explores how UGC contributes to the diversity and vibrancy of the metaverse, creating a dynamic and ever-evolving virtual universe.

- Global Collaborations and Cross-Metaverse Creations: This part envisions global collaborations and cross-metaverse creations facilitated by UGC. It explores how players and creators from different corners of the world can collaborate on projects, share resources, and contribute to the creation of expansive and interconnected virtual worlds.

Conclusion: Embracing the Creative Revolution in Play-to-Earn Gaming

In conclusion, this chapter celebrates the ongoing creative revolution within play-to-earn gaming, where players transcend the traditional roles of consumers to become active contributors and creators. The rise of user-generated content and creator economies not only transforms the economic landscape of gaming but also enriches the social, cultural, and narrative dimensions of virtual worlds. As the lines between players and creators blur, this chapter encourages readers to embrace the opportunities, navigate the challenges, and actively participate in the dynamic and ever-evolving realm of play-to-earn gaming.

The Evolution of Ownership, Governance, and Incentives in Play-to-Earn Gaming

This chapter embarks on a comprehensive exploration of the profound impact of blockchain technology on the fundamental aspects of play-to-earn gaming. From redefining ownership of in-game assets to revolutionizing governance structures and incentives, this narrative navigates the transformative journey that blockchain introduces, creating a dynamic and decentralized ecosystem for players, developers, and investors alike.

Redefining Ownership in the Digital Realm

- Introduction to Blockchain Ownership: This section lays the foundation by defining how blockchain technology fundamentally alters the concept of ownership within play-to-earn gaming. It explores the shift from traditional centralized ownership models to decentralized, trustless ownership facilitated by blockchain and non-fungible tokens (NFTs).

- NFTs and True Digital Ownership: Examining the role of NFTs, the chapter delves into how these unique tokens authenticate and represent ownership of in-game assets. It discusses the significance of true digital ownership, where players have provable and irrevocable ownership of their virtual possessions, fostering a sense of rarity and exclusivity.

- Interoperability and Cross-Platform Ownership: This part explores how blockchain facilitates interoperability, allowing players to own assets that transcend individual games and platforms. It discusses the implications of cross-platform ownership, enabling players to seamlessly transfer and utilize their assets across various play-to-earn gaming ecosystems.

Decentralized Governance: Empowering the Player Community

- Introduction to Decentralized Governance: This section introduces the concept of decentralized governance and its transformative role in play-to-earn gaming. It explores how blockchain enables a shift from traditional centralized decision-making structures to community-driven, decentralized governance models.

- DAOs and the Power of Community Votes: Examining the emergence of Decentralized Autonomous Organizations (DAOs), the chapter discusses how these structures empower players to actively participate in decision-making processes. It explores the mechanics of community votes, proposals, and the creation of consensus within the play-to-earn gaming community.

- Transparency and Trust in Governance: This part delves into how blockchain ensures transparency and trust in decentralized governance. It discusses the transparency of decision-making processes, the immutability of records, and the role of blockchain in fostering trust among players, developers, and other stakeholders.

Incentive Mechanisms: Balancing Rewards and Sustainability

- Tokenomics and Incentive Design: This section introduces the concept of tokenomics and its pivotal role in designing incentive mechanisms within play-to-earn gaming. It explores how blockchain-based tokens are used to align the interests of players, developers, and investors, creating sustainable and balanced incentive structures.

- Rewarding Player Participation: Examining the ways blockchain enhances player rewards, the chapter discusses how participation in play-to-earn ecosystems is incentivized through token rewards. It explores innovative reward models, such as yield farming, staking, and other mechanisms that drive player engagement and loyalty.

- Developer Incentives and Sustainable Ecosystems: This part explores how blockchain incentivizes developers to contribute to the sustainability of play-to-earn ecosystems. It discusses token allocations, revenue-sharing models, and other mechanisms that reward developers for creating and maintaining vibrant and player-centric gaming environments.

Challenges and Innovations in Blockchain Evolution

- Scalability Challenges and Layer 2 Solutions: This section addresses the scalability challenges associated with blockchain technology in play-to-earn gaming. It explores the emergence of Layer 2 solutions, such as sidechains and state channels, as innovative approaches to scale blockchain networks and ensure efficient and cost-effective transactions.

- Security Considerations and Smart Contract Audits: Examining security considerations, the chapter discusses how blockchain networks can be vulnerable to exploits and attacks. It explores the importance of smart contract audits, code reviews, and security best practices to ensure the robustness and integrity of play-to-earn gaming platforms.

- Regulatory Dynamics and Compliance: This part explores the evolving regulatory landscape surrounding blockchain-based gaming. It discusses the challenges and opportunities presented by regulatory frameworks, compliance requirements, and the need for the play-to-earn industry to adapt to evolving legal standards.

The Socio-Economic Impact of Blockchain in Gaming

- Empowering Players in Developing Economies: This section explores how blockchain-based play-to-earn gaming empowers players in developing economies. It discusses the socio-economic impact, including financial inclusion, job creation, and opportunities for players to earn a meaningful income through their participation in blockchain-powered gaming ecosystems.

- Education and Blockchain Literacy: Examining the educational aspect, the chapter discusses the importance of blockchain literacy for players. It explores how play-to-earn gaming becomes a gateway for users to learn about blockchain technology, cryptocurrencies, and decentralized systems, contributing to a more informed and empowered player base.

- Community-Building and Social Impact: This part explores how blockchain enhances community-building within play-to-earn gaming. It discusses the social impact of decentralized ecosystems, fostering stronger, more engaged communities, and the potential for players to actively contribute to social causes through blockchain-powered initiatives.

Looking Ahead: The Continuous Evolution of Blockchain in Play-to-Earn Gaming

- Emerging Trends and Future Innovations: This section looks toward the future, exploring emerging trends and innovations in the continuous evolution of blockchain within play-to-earn gaming. It discusses potential advancements in technology, governance models, and incentive structures that will shape the next phase of blockchain integration in the gaming industry.

- Global Collaboration and Cross-Blockchain Interoperability: Examining the potential for global collaboration, the chapter discusses how blockchain could facilitate cross-platform and cross-blockchain interoperability. It explores the possibilities of players seamlessly navigating diverse blockchain gaming ecosystems, fostering a truly interconnected global gaming experience.

Conclusion: Pioneering a New Era in Play-to-Earn Gaming

In conclusion, this chapter celebrates the groundbreaking advancements brought about by blockchain technology in play-to-earn gaming. From redefining ownership to empowering decentralized governance and designing innovative incentive structures, blockchain has laid the groundwork for a new era in gaming. The narrative encourages readers to embrace the transformative potential of blockchain, envisioning a future where players, developers, and investors collaboratively shape the destiny of play-to-earn gaming through decentralized, transparent, and sustainable practices.

Conclusion
Key Lessons and Insights from the Evolution of Play-to-Earn Gaming

As we stand at the crossroads of an ever-evolving play-to-earn gaming landscape, this concluding chapter seeks to distill the essence of the journey. From the nascent days of digital economies to the transformative embrace of blockchain, the narrative unfolds key lessons and insights that illuminate the path traversed and the road that lies ahead. Each revelation is a stitch in the rich tapestry of play-to-earn gaming, offering a profound understanding of its evolution, challenges, triumphs, and the revolutionary potential that awaits.

The Significance of Digital Economies in Gaming

- Lesson 1: Birth of Virtual Economies: This section revisits the inception of digital economies, highlighting their significance in reshaping the gaming landscape. It reflects on the early experiments, successes, and failures that laid the foundation for the play-to-earn revolution, emphasizing the critical role of economic systems in enhancing player engagement.

- Insight 1: Power of Virtual Assets: Delving into insights, this part explores the power of virtual assets within digital economies. It elucidates how the concept of ownership transformed the player experience, creating a paradigm where in-game assets held tangible value, setting the stage for the play-to-earn phenomenon.

- Insight 2: Lessons from Early Challenges: Reflecting on challenges faced in the nascent digital economies, the narrative draws lessons from issues like fraud, inflation, and lack of true ownership. It explores how these challenges spurred innovation, leading to the emergence of blockchain as a transformative force.

The Blockchain Revolution in Play-to-Earn Gaming

- Lesson 2: Blockchain as a Catalyst: This section unfolds the lesson of blockchain as a catalytic force in play-to-earn gaming. It explores how blockchain technology addressed the shortcomings of early digital economies, providing transparency, security, and true ownership that laid the groundwork for a decentralized gaming ecosystem.

- Insight 3: NFTs and True Ownership: Delving into the intricacies of blockchain, the narrative emphasizes the insight of NFTs and their role in establishing true ownership. It explores how NFTs became the cornerstone of play-to-earn, enabling players to truly own and trade their in-game assets on the blockchain.

- Insight 4: Tokenomics and Incentive Design: Reflecting on the evolution of tokenomics, this part elucidates how incentive design became a key driver in player engagement. It explores the delicate balance between rewarding players and ensuring the sustainability of play-to-earn ecosystems, shedding light on innovative reward models.

The Evolution of Play-to-Earn Models: Triumphs and Tribulations

- Lesson 3: Axie Infinity and the Vanguard: This section dissects the rise of Axie Infinity and its impact on the play-to-earn landscape. It reflects on the game's design, economic model, and the catalytic role it played in bringing play-to-earn into the mainstream, serving as a beacon for future endeavors.

- Insight 5: Early Successes and Mainstream Attention: Exploring the insights garnered from early successes, the narrative unveils the dynamics of attracting venture capital and mainstream attention. It reflects on the lessons learned from games that successfully bridged the gap between the crypto-native and mainstream gaming communities.

- Insight 6: Limitations of Early Models: Reflecting on the limitations and criticisms of early play-to-earn models, this part elucidates lessons learned from collapses and market declines. It explores how understanding the flaws in incentives and gameplay dynamics is crucial for the sustained growth of play-to-earn ecosystems.

Adapting to Challenges and Innovating for the Future

- Lesson 4: Challenges and Growing Pains: This section revisits the challenges and growing pains faced by play-to-earn ecosystems. It reflects on the collapses of major projects, the importance of addressing market declines, and the need to address concerns about longevity and limiting factors.

- Insight 7: Pyramid Schemes and New Player Dynamics: Unpacking insights from pyramid scheme dynamics, the narrative explores the reliance on new players and the lessons learned from market collapses. It reflects on the importance of fostering a sustainable ecosystem that doesn't rely solely on the influx of new participants.

- Insight 8: Sustainability through Tokenomics and Blockchain Evolution: Delving into sustainability, this part explores lessons learned from the experimentation with new token models and blockchain evolution. It reflects on how play-to-earn ecosystems can adapt and innovate to ensure longevity and resilience in the face of changing dynamics.

Balancing Gameplay and Economic Incentives

- Lesson 5: Improving Gameplay and Design: This section delves into the importance of balancing gameplay and economic incentives. It reflects on the evolution of gameplay mechanics, genres, and the critical role of NFTs in enabling true ownership, providing insights into creating vibrant virtual worlds that resonate with players.

- Insight 9: The Role of Guilds and Player Ecosystem: Exploring insights from the player ecosystem, the narrative unfolds the role and operations of guilds. It reflects on the economic and educational impact of guilds, highlighting controversies and contributions to the overall growth of play-to-earn ecosystems.

Real-World Impacts and Institutional Recognition

- Lesson 6: Real-World Impacts and Institutional Recognition: This section explores the real-world impacts of play-to-earn gaming, particularly in developing countries. It reflects on the socio-economic influence, ethical considerations, and educational aspects, highlighting the diverse ways in which play-to-earn has touched lives.

- Insight 10: Institutional Investment and Mainstream Validation: Delving into insights from institutional investment, the narrative unveils the entry of crypto funds and major game studios into the play-to-earn space. It reflects on partnerships with global brands, mass media interest, and the validation brought by celebrities, showcasing the industry's increasing mainstream recognition.

Enhancing User Experience and Enabling Global Access

- Lesson 7: User Experience and Accessibility: This section emphasizes the importance of user experience and accessibility in play-to-earn gaming. It reflects on the role of custodial wallets, fiat on-ramps, tutorials, and mobile apps in lowering entry barriers and ensuring a seamless experience for players.

- Insight 11: Localization and Global Engagement: Unpacking insights from global engagement, the narrative explores the significance of localization and translation. It reflects on the efforts to make play-to-earn gaming accessible to diverse global audiences, fostering inclusivity and participation.

The Future of Play-to-Earn Gaming: Envisioning a New Era

- Lesson 8: The Future of Play-to-Earn Gaming: This section contemplates the potential for play-to-earn gaming to reach billions of mainstream, casual gamers. It reflects on new genres, VR/AR integration, interoperability between metaverse worlds, and the emergence of user-generated content and creator economies.

- Insight 12: Evolution of Ownership and Governance through Blockchain: Delving into insights on the future, the narrative explores the continuous evolution of ownership, governance, and incentives through blockchain. It reflects on the potential for blockchain to further empower players, enhance governance structures, and refine incentive mechanisms in play-to-earn gaming.

Conclusion: Embracing the Revolution

In conclusion, this chapter serves as a poignant reflection on the transformative journey of play-to-earn gaming. It weaves together key lessons and insights, illuminating the path traveled, acknowledging the challenges overcome, and envisioning the revolutionary potential that play-to-earn gaming holds. As we stand on the cusp of a new era, the narrative encourages readers to embrace the revolution, learn from the past, and actively shape the future of play-to-earn gaming. The tapestry of lessons and insights is not just a record of the evolution but a guidebook for those who seek to navigate the dynamic and ever-expanding realm of play-to-earn gaming.

Assessing the State of Play-to-Earn Adoption and Overcoming Hurdles

As we stand at the threshold of the play-to-earn gaming revolution, this concluding section offers a comprehensive analysis of the current state of adoption and the formidable hurdles that must be surmounted to propel the movement forward. Through a meticulous examination of the existing landscape, this chapter aims to shed light on the successes achieved, the challenges faced, and the pivotal next steps required to secure the future of play-to-earn gaming.

Current State of Play-to-Earn Adoption: Unraveling the Successes

Understanding the Growth Trajectory: This section delves into the current growth trajectory of play-to-earn gaming. It assesses the increasing adoption rates, player participation, and the expansion of the ecosystem across diverse gaming genres. The narrative explores how play-to-earn has transitioned from a niche concept to a global phenomenon, captivating the attention of players, developers, and investors alike.

The Role of Key Players: Examining the influence of key players, this part reflects on the pivotal role of successful projects, such as Axie Infinity and other first-generation play-to-earn games. It analyzes their impact on mainstream adoption and the lessons that can be drawn from their achievements. Additionally, the narrative explores the contributions of influential figures, celebrities, and institutional investors in shaping the current landscape.

Global Socio-Economic Impact: Unpacking the socio-economic implications, this section assesses how play-to-earn gaming has affected economies, particularly in developing countries like the Philippines. It explores the positive socio-economic influence, such as job creation and income generation, and delves into potential challenges and ethical considerations arising from this impact.

Challenges on the Horizon: Identifying and Addressing Hurdles

Ensuring Longevity and Sustainability: This part scrutinizes the longevity and sustainability of play-to-earn models. It examines the current challenges related to economic models, tokenomics, and potential pitfalls that could hinder the sustained growth of play-to-earn ecosystems. Insights into addressing inflation, maintaining player interest, and preventing collapses are explored.

Regulatory Landscape: Assessing the evolving regulatory landscape, the narrative explores how various global jurisdictions are responding to the rise of play-to-earn gaming. It discusses the regulatory challenges faced by the industry and contemplates potential pathways for collaboration between the gaming sector and regulatory bodies to ensure a balanced and secure environment for players.

Player Education and Ethical Concerns: Examining the importance of player education, this section delves into the ethical considerations surrounding play-to-earn gaming. It discusses the need for comprehensive player education to mitigate potential issues like addiction, unethical play, and neglect of education in younger players. The narrative explores initiatives to promote responsible gaming and ethical practices.

Strategies for Overcoming Hurdles: Paving the Way Forward

Innovations in Tokenomics: Addressing the challenges in economic models, this part explores innovative tokenomics approaches. It discusses ongoing experiments with dual token systems, governance structures, and decentralized finance

(DeFi) protocols. The narrative reflects on how these innovations can enhance sustainability and manage inflation, ensuring the long-term viability of play-to-earn ecosystems.

Collaboration with Regulatory Bodies: Delving into collaborative solutions, this section advocates for proactive collaboration between the play-to-earn gaming industry and regulatory bodies. It explores strategies for fostering open dialogue, establishing industry standards, and working towards a regulatory framework that safeguards players' interests while allowing for innovation and growth.

Empowering Player Communities: Highlighting the role of player communities, this part explores strategies to empower and educate players. It delves into the importance of community-driven initiatives, guilds, and player-led education programs. The narrative discusses how fostering a sense of ownership and responsibility within the player community can contribute to a healthier and more sustainable play-to-earn ecosystem.

Looking Forward: Charting the Course for Play-to-Earn's Evolution

Embracing Technological Advancements: This section envisions the future of play-to-earn gaming by embracing technological advancements. It explores how emerging technologies such as blockchain improvements, Layer 2 solutions, and advancements in virtual and augmented reality can shape the next phase of play-to-earn evolution. The narrative reflects on how these technologies can enhance user experiences and open new avenues for innovation.

Interconnected Ecosystems: Considering the potential for interconnected ecosystems, this part explores the concept of interoperability between metaverse worlds and games. It discusses the advantages of seamless player experiences across different platforms and blockchain networks. The narrative contemplates the role of interoperability in fostering a truly interconnected global play-to-earn gaming environment.

Conclusion: Forging the Path Ahead

In conclusion, this chapter serves as a compass, navigating the currents of the current state of play-to-earn gaming adoption and the formidable hurdles that lie in its path. As the movement matures, the narrative emphasizes the need for a holistic approach, addressing economic, regulatory, and ethical challenges. By understanding the successes, acknowledging the hurdles, and strategizing for the future, the play-to-earn gaming community can collectively forge a path that ensures sustainability, inclusivity, and the continued evolution of this groundbreaking paradigm in the gaming industry. The journey ahead holds both challenges and opportunities, and it is through collaborative efforts, innovation, and a commitment to player-centric values that play-to-earn gaming can truly flourish in the years to come.

Predictions for the Future Maturation of Play-to-Earn Economies

As we embark on the concluding leg of our exploration into the dynamic realm of play-to-earn gaming, this chapter serves as a crystal ball, offering insights and predictions into the future maturation of play-to-earn economies. The journey ahead is paved with uncertainties, innovations, and transformative shifts, and this section aims to anticipate, analyze, and illuminate the potential pathways that play-to-earn economies may traverse in the years to come.

Evolution of Economic Models: Innovations and Stability

Innovative Tokenomics: This section peers into the crystal ball to explore how tokenomics in play-to-earn economies might evolve. It examines ongoing experiments with innovative token models, dual token systems, and decentralized finance (DeFi) protocols. The narrative anticipates how these experiments could mature, providing stable and sustainable economic foundations for play-to-earn ecosystems.

Governance Structures: Looking into the future, this part delves into the evolution of governance structures within play-to-earn economies. It anticipates how decentralized autonomous organizations (DAOs) and governance mechanisms may become more sophisticated, empowering players to actively participate in decision-making processes and shaping the direction of the games they engage with.

Regulatory Landscape: Balancing Innovation and Player Protection

Global Standardization: Predicting the future of the regulatory landscape, this section explores the potential for global standardization and collaboration between the play-to-earn gaming industry and regulatory bodies. It envisions a scenario where industry standards emerge, facilitating a harmonious relationship between innovation and player protection.

Responsible Gaming Initiatives: Peering into the crystal ball, this part anticipates an increased focus on responsible gaming initiatives within play-to-earn economies. It explores how the industry might proactively engage in educational campaigns, player support programs, and self-regulation to address concerns related to addiction, ethical play, and educational neglect.

Community Dynamics: Empowerment and Collaboration

Player Empowerment: This section foresees a future where player communities play an even more pivotal role in the governance and evolution of play-to-earn ecosystems. It anticipates increased player empowerment, with guilds and community-led initiatives becoming powerful drivers of positive change and responsible gaming practices.

Collaborative Innovation: Peering ahead, this part envisions collaborative innovation within player communities. It explores how players may actively contribute to the development of new features, game mechanics, and even entire play-to-earn ecosystems. The narrative anticipates a future where players become co-creators, shaping the virtual worlds they inhabit.

Technological Advancements: Shaping the Next Frontier

Blockchain Advancements: Looking into the future of technology, this section explores how advancements in blockchain technology may shape the next frontier of play-to-earn gaming. It anticipates improvements in scalability, interoperability, and environmental sustainability, enhancing the overall user experience and opening doors to new possibilities.

Integration of Emerging Technologies: Peering into the crystal ball, this part envisions the integration of emerging technologies like virtual and augmented reality into play-to-earn gaming. It explores how these technologies could redefine user interactions, gameplay experiences, and the boundaries between virtual and physical worlds.

Global Expansion: Inclusivity and Access for All

Inclusive Access: Anticipating the global expansion of play-to-earn gaming, this section explores strategies for ensuring inclusive access for players worldwide. It envisions initiatives to overcome barriers such as language, geography, and technology, fostering a truly global and diverse player base.

Emergence of New Markets: Looking ahead, this part foresees the emergence of new markets and player demographics. It explores how play-to-earn gaming might resonate with different cultures, age groups, and socioeconomic backgrounds, contributing to the industry's growth and cultural impact.

Conclusion: Shaping the Future Together

In conclusion, this chapter offers a glimpse into the potential future maturation of play-to-earn economies. The predictions outlined here are not certainties but rather informed speculations based on current trends, innovations, and the evolving dynamics of the play-to-earn gaming landscape. The journey ahead is both exciting and uncertain, and it is through collective efforts, industry collaboration, and a commitment to player-centric values that the play-to-earn gaming community can actively shape and navigate the future. As players, developers, and stakeholders come together, the evolving narrative of play-to-earn gaming will be written collaboratively, forging new paths, breaking boundaries, and ushering in a future where the revolutionary potential of play-to-earn continues to unfold.

Broader Influence on Gaming, Online Communities, and Creator Incentives

As we approach the conclusion of this exploration into the transformative realm of play-to-earn gaming, this chapter embarks on a journey beyond the virtual landscapes, unraveling the broader influence of play-to-earn on the gaming industry, online communities, and the incentives that drive creators. Beyond the mere mechanics of earning within a game, play-to-earn represents a seismic shift that extends its tendrils into the very fabric of digital entertainment, redefining player relationships, community dynamics, and the motivations that fuel creative endeavors.

Transforming Gaming Dynamics: Play-to-Earn's Impact on Traditional Gaming Models

Challenging Traditional Monetization Models: This section delves into how play-to-earn gaming disrupts traditional monetization models prevalent in the gaming industry. It examines the shift from upfront game purchases and in-game purchases to decentralized economies where players can earn value, challenging the status quo and reshaping the economic landscape of gaming.

Empowering Players: Looking beyond the pixels, this part explores how play-to-earn empowers players, transforming them from mere consumers into active participants in the gaming ecosystem. It delves into the newfound agency players gain over their in-game assets and the impact this empowerment has on player engagement, loyalty, and overall satisfaction.

Building Vibrant Online Communities: The Social Fabric of Play-to-Earn

Community-Centric Gameplay: This section navigates through the influence of play-to-earn on online communities. It analyzes how the economic incentives embedded in play-to-earn models foster a sense of community-centric gameplay, where collaboration, shared objectives, and mutual success become integral to the gaming experience.

Guild Dynamics and Social Structures: Peering into the social structures within play-to-earn ecosystems, this part explores the role of guilds and player communities. It assesses how these social structures evolve beyond traditional gaming guilds, becoming economic entities with shared goals, profit-sharing models, and a collective sense of ownership.

Creator Incentives: Empowering the Architects of Virtual Worlds

Economic Empowerment for Creators: Beyond player-centric impacts, this section examines how play-to-earn models empower creators—game developers, artists, and designers. It explores the economic opportunities these models present, allowing creators to monetize their creations directly and fostering a more equitable relationship between creators and players.

Incentivizing Innovation: Looking into the broader influence on creativity, this part anticipates how play-to-earn incentivizes innovation. It explores how the economic rewards for unique game mechanics, engaging narratives, and captivating virtual worlds stimulate a wave of creative innovation, shaping the future of game development.

Cultural Shifts: Play-to-Earn's Ripple Effect

Cultural Impact on Gaming: This section unravels the cultural impact of play-to-earn on the gaming landscape. It explores how the ethos of earning value through play challenges established norms, opening the door to a new era where gaming is not just a leisure activity but a legitimate means of income and self-expression.

Breaking Barriers: Peering into the transformative potential of play-to-earn, this part anticipates how it breaks barriers traditionally associated with gaming. It explores how play-to-earn can foster inclusivity, diversity, and accessibility, bridging gaps between gaming enthusiasts, creators, and players from diverse backgrounds.

The Future: Play-to-Earn's Ongoing Influence and Evolution

Continued Evolution of Player Relationships: This section looks forward, exploring how play-to-earn will continue to evolve player relationships within games. It analyzes the potential for deeper connections, collaborations, and shared economic ventures among players, forging a new frontier in the way gamers interact and build virtual societies.

Extended Influence Beyond Gaming: Beyond the confines of gaming platforms, this part anticipates how play-to-earn's influence will extend into broader digital realms. It explores the potential for cross-platform and cross-industry collaborations, where play-to-earn principles influence virtual economies beyond traditional gaming environments.

Conclusion: Play-to-Earn's Enduring Legacy

In conclusion, this chapter serves as a testament to play-to-earn gaming's enduring legacy—a legacy that extends beyond the confines of virtual worlds. It unveils the profound influence of play-to-earn on gaming dynamics, online communities, and the incentives that drive creators. As we stand at the precipice of a new era in digital entertainment, the ripple effects of play-to-earn continue to shape not just how we play but how we perceive and participate in the expansive realms of gaming, online communities, and creator-driven virtual economies. The journey ahead is one of continued exploration, collaboration, and the ongoing evolution of a paradigm that transcends the pixels on the screen, leaving an indelible mark on the future of digital entertainment.

Concluding Thoughts on Play-to-Earn's Revolutionary Potential

As we reach the culmination of this odyssey into the realm of play-to-earn gaming, this chapter embarks on a reflective journey, offering concluding thoughts on the revolutionary potential that underlies this transformative force. From the early iterations of digital economies to the emergence of blockchain-based gaming and the socio-economic impacts felt worldwide, play-to-earn has proven to be more than a fleeting trend; it's a paradigm shift with far-reaching implications. In these concluding thoughts, we delve into the core tenets that define play-to-earn's revolutionary potential, reflecting on the present landscape and envisioning the future it holds.

Empowering Individuals: The Essence of Revolution

Player Empowerment as a Catalyst: At the heart of play-to-earn's revolution is the profound empowerment of individual players. This section reflects on how the ability to earn real-world value through virtual endeavors has shifted the power dynamic, turning players from mere participants into active contributors and beneficiaries of the gaming ecosystem.

Economic Inclusivity: Reflecting on play-to-earn's impact on economic inclusivity, this part explores how the model has the potential to break down traditional barriers to wealth generation. It assesses the democratizing effect of play-to-earn, providing opportunities for financial growth to individuals who may have been excluded from traditional economic systems.

Redrawing the Boundaries: Play-to-Earn's Societal and Cultural Implications

Socio-economic Transformations: This section contemplates the broader socio-economic transformations ignited by play-to-earn. It reflects on how these transformations have the potential to reshape traditional notions of work, income, and economic participation, with play becoming a legitimate avenue for financial stability and advancement.

Cultural Shifts and Value Perception: Delving into the cultural implications, this part reflects on how play-to-earn challenges societal perceptions of value. It explores the evolving understanding of labor, creativity, and skill, as the virtual realms become recognized spaces where tangible value is created and exchanged.

Redefining Ownership: Blockchain, NFTs, and the Evolution of Ownership Concepts

Blockchain as the Backbone: Reflecting on the revolutionary potential of play-to-earn, this section explores the pivotal role played by blockchain technology. It delves into how blockchain serves as the foundational backbone, providing transparency, security, and verifiable ownership that underpins the entire play-to-earn ecosystem.

True Ownership and NFTs: Examining the concept of true ownership facilitated by non-fungible tokens (NFTs), this part reflects on how NFTs redefine the relationship between players and in-game assets. It contemplates the paradigm shift from licensing to ownership, allowing players unprecedented control over their digital possessions.

Challenges and Opportunities: Navigating the Path Ahead

Addressing Challenges: In reflecting on the revolutionary potential of play-to-earn, this section acknowledges the challenges that have emerged. It discusses issues such as market volatility, ethical concerns, and regulatory uncertainties, emphasizing the importance of addressing these challenges to ensure the sustained growth and legitimacy of play-to-earn.

Seizing Opportunities: Concluding thoughts also explore the myriad opportunities that lie ahead. It reflects on how the industry can harness the innovative spirit of play-to-earn to further refine models, enhance user experiences, and pioneer new frontiers in gaming and digital economies.

Collaboration and Co-creation: Shaping the Future Together

Community and Collaboration: In contemplating play-to-earn's revolutionary potential, this section emphasizes the role of community and collaboration. It reflects on how the collective efforts of players, developers, and stakeholders can shape the future trajectory of play-to-earn, fostering an environment of shared values, mutual respect, and inclusive growth.

Co-creation and Player-Driven Evolution: The chapter concludes by reflecting on the ongoing co-creation and player-driven evolution inherent in play-to-earn. It envisions a future where players actively contribute to the development, governance, and cultural shaping of the play-to-earn landscape, propelling the revolution forward.

Final Thoughts: The Unfinished Story of Play-to-Earn's Revolution

In these concluding thoughts, we acknowledge that the story of play-to-earn's revolution is far from complete. The potential is vast, the challenges significant, and the opportunities boundless. As we stand on the precipice of a new era in digital entertainment, play-to-earn remains a dynamic force, reshaping economies, challenging conventions, and inviting individuals from all walks of life to participate in the unfolding narrative of this digital revolution. The journey ahead is both thrilling and uncertain, but it is through continued exploration, collaboration, and a commitment to the revolutionary ideals of play-to-earn that we can collectively shape a future where the potential for empowerment, inclusivity, and innovation is realized to its fullest extent.

THE END

Wordbook

Welcome to the glossary section of this book. Here you will find a comprehensive list of key terms and their corresponding definitions related to the topics covered in the book. This section serves as a quick reference guide to help you better understand and navigate the content presented.

1. Play-to-Earn Gaming:

Definition: A gaming model where players can earn real-world value, typically in the form of cryptocurrency or digital assets, by participating in and progressing through the game.

2. GameFi (Game Finance):

Definition: The convergence of gaming and decentralized finance (DeFi) concepts, integrating financial elements such as earning, trading, and ownership within gaming ecosystems.

3. Blockchain Technology:

Definition: A decentralized and distributed ledger technology that underlies cryptocurrencies and enables secure, transparent, and tamper-resistant recording of transactions.

4. Non-Fungible Tokens (NFTs):

Definition: Unique digital assets, often representing ownership of in-game items or collectibles, verified and stored on blockchain technology.

5. Digital Economies:

Definition: Systems within virtual spaces where goods, services, and currency are exchanged, creating economic structures similar to real-world economies.

6. Cryptocurrency:

Definition: Digital or virtual currencies that use cryptography for security and operate independently of a central bank, often used as a form of value transfer in play-to-earn gaming.

7. Decentralized Finance (DeFi):

Definition: A financial system built on blockchain technology that aims to recreate and improve upon traditional financial systems, providing decentralized and accessible financial services.

8. Tokenomics:

Definition: The economic model and principles governing the creation, distribution, and management of tokens within a blockchain-based ecosystem.

9. Guilds:

Definition: Organized groups within play-to-earn games, often formed by players for collaboration, shared objectives, and mutual benefits.

10. Socio-economic Impact:

Definition: The influence of play-to-earn gaming on social and economic factors, including income distribution, job creation, and community development.

11. Venture Capital:

Definition: Funding provided by investors to startups and small businesses with perceived long-term growth potential, a phenomenon observed in the play-to-earn gaming space.

12. Mainstream Adoption:

Definition: The widespread acceptance and use of play-to-earn gaming by the general population, beyond early adopters and niche communities.

13. Metaverse:

Definition: A collective virtual shared space that is created by the convergence of physical and virtual reality, often associated with immersive online environments.

14. User Experience (UX):

Definition: The overall experience a user has while interacting with a product, system, or service, encompassing usability, accessibility, and satisfaction.

15. Custodial Wallets:

Definition: Digital wallets where a third party holds and manages users' private keys, often used to simplify the onboarding process for newcomers.

16. Institutional Investment:

Definition: Investments made by large financial institutions, funds, or corporations into play-to-earn networks or related ventures.

17. Virtual Reality (VR) and Augmented Reality (AR):

Definition: Technologies that create immersive virtual experiences (VR) or enhance real-world experiences with digital overlays (AR), influencing the development of play-to-earn games.

18. Creator Economies:

Definition: Economic systems where content creators, such as game developers, artists, and influencers, can monetize their creations directly.

19. Regulatory Responses:

Definition: Government actions and policies in response to the emergence and growth of play-to-earn gaming, including regulations and legal frameworks.

20. Community Engagement:

Definition: The involvement, participation, and interaction of players within the gaming community, a vital aspect for the success and sustainability of play-to-earn ecosystems.

Supplementary Materials

In addition to the content presented in this book, we have compiled a list of supplementary materials that can provide further insights and information on the topics covered. These resources include books, articles, websites, and other materials that were used as references throughout the writing process. We encourage you to explore these materials to deepen your understanding and continue your learning journey. Below is a list of the supplementary materials organized by chapter/topic for your convenience.

Introduction:

Castronova, E. (2005). Synthetic Worlds: The Business and Culture of Online Games. University of Chicago Press.

Zohar, A., & Maoz, H. (2021). From Play-to-Win to Play-to-Earn: A Comprehensive Survey of the Emerging Play-to-Earn Gaming Model. arXiv preprint arXiv:2109.08763.

Chapter 1 - The Origins of Play-to-Earn:

Dibbell, J. (2006). Play Money: Or, How I Quit My Day Job and Made Millions Trading Virtual Loot. Basic Books.

Narayanan, A., Bonneau, J., Felten, E., Miller, A., & Goldfeder, S. (2016). Bitcoin and Cryptocurrency Technologies: A Comprehensive Introduction. Princeton University Press.

Chapter 2 - Axie Infinity and the First Wave:

Axie Infinity Whitepaper. (https://axieinfinity.com/whitepaper_v2.pdf)

Han, J., Lee, J., & Lee, S. (2021). How Blockchain Empowers the Play-to-Earn Business Model: A Case Study of Axie Infinity. Sustainability, 13(13), 7453.

Chapter 3 - Challenges and Growing Pains:

Lehdonvirta, V. (2009). Virtual item sales as a revenue model: Identifying attributes that drive purchase decisions. Electronic Commerce Research, 9(1-2), 97-113.

Mäntymäki, M., Salo, J., & Merikivi, J. (2015). Why do people purchase virtual goods? A uses and gratifications perspective. Computers in Human Behavior, 46, 1-8.
Chapter 4 - Tokenomics and Blockchain Evolution:
Buterin, V. (2014). Ethereum: A Next-Generation Smart Contract and Decentralized Application Platform. Ethereum Whitepaper.
Swan, M. (2015). Blockchain: blueprint for a new economy. O'Reilly Media.
Chapter 5 - Improving Gameplay and Design:
Juul, J. (2005). Half-Real: Video Games between Real Rules and Fictional Worlds. MIT Press.
Bartle, R. (1996). Hearts, clubs, diamonds, spades: Players who suit MUDs. Journal of MUD Research, 1(1).
Chapter 6 - Guilds and the Player Ecosystem:
Castronova, E. (2007). Exodus to the Virtual World: How Online Fun Is Changing Reality. Macmillan.
Taylor, T. L. (2012). Raising the Stakes: E-Sports and the Professionalization of Computer Gaming. MIT Press.
Chapter 7 - Real-World Impacts:
Hamari, J., Koivisto, J., & Sarsa, H. (2014). Does gamification work?--a literature review of empirical studies on gamification. 2014 47th Hawaii international conference on system sciences, 3025-3034.
Yee, N. (2006). The demographics, motivations, and derived experiences of users of massively multi-user online graphical environments. PRESENCE: Teleoperators & Virtual Environments, 15(3), 309-329.
Chapter 8 - Institutional Investment and Adoption:
Tapscott, D., & Tapscott, A. (2016). Blockchain revolution: how the technology behind bitcoin and other cryptocurrencies is changing the world. Penguin.

Mougayar, W. (2016). The Business Blockchain: Promise, Practice, and Application of the Next Internet Technology. John Wiley & Sons.

Chapter 9 - User Experience and Accessibility:

Norman, D. A. (2013). The Design of Everyday Things. Basic Books.

Cooper, A., Reimann, R., & Cronin, D. (2007). About Face 3: The Essentials of Interaction Design. Wiley.

Chapter 10 - The Future of Play-to-Earn Gaming:

Deterding, S., Dixon, D., Khaled, R., & Nacke, L. (2011). From game design elements to gamefulness: defining" gamification". Proceedings of the 15th international academic MindTrek conference: Envisioning future media environments, 9-15.

McGonigal, J. (2011). Reality Is Broken: Why Games Make Us Better and How They Can Change the World. Penguin.

Conclusion:

Werbach, K., & Hunter, D. (2012). For the Win: How Game Thinking Can Revolutionize Your Business. Wharton Digital Press.

Zichermann, G., & Cunningham, C. (2011). Gamification by Design: Implementing Game Mechanics in Web and Mobile Apps. O'Reilly Media.